HUNGER FOR REALITY

GEORGE VERWER

LITERATURE

Dedicated to

John Watts and Keith Beckwith

members of Operation Mobilization who encouraged me to put this message into print and who died in an auto crash in Poland in 1965 while fulfilling the Great Commission committed to them by the Lord Jesus Christ.

Second edition 1977
Reprinted 1979, 1981, 1983, 1986, 1989
This edition reprinted 1997

Acknowledgement:
The quotations by A.W. Tozer are taken from *The Pursuit of God* and *Of God and Men*, reprinted by kind permission of Christian Publications, Camp Hill, PA 17001, U.S.A.

ISBN: 18845-4307-3

OM Literature
P.O. Box 1047
Waynesboro, GA 30830-2047
U.S.A.

Printed in Colombia

BUENA SEMILLA
Apartado 29724
Bogotá, Colombia

Contents

Introduction

Farewell to Schizophrenia

No one could say in these days that we Christians are spiritually starved. Through the care and faithfulness of God's servants, we are generously fed, taught, encouraged, pampered, stimulated, supported, nursed along. A religious world of sermons, discussions, magazine articles, hymns, messages, books, meetings, and conferences surrounds us for our participation and growth. Yet we know very well, if we are honest, that these things have all too little effect on our lives. Why is this so?

If we give the matter a little thought, we will realize that most of us are living in "two worlds." We have split our convictions, activities, and goals into two categories. In the first we place our religious experiences: what we believe; what we sing about; what we pray about; and what we defend in argument.

The second category contains our world of secular values and actions: our use of leisure time; our actions taken to impress people; our attitude towards associates who are better or worse at their job than we are; and how we get our money and use it.

We keep these two worlds strictly apart, and though we may vaguely feel that something is wrong, we don't suspect we are suffering a major disorder — a sort of spiritual schizophrenia. In church, and occasionally among Christian friends, we talk about dedication, commitment, surrender, revival, a life on fire for God, and other expressions of loyalty and love for God. But the words and their corresponding deeds get little exposure outside church walls.

This evangelical dichotomy has had more serious results than we admit. It has produced men who are hard to get along with, women who rank themselves by the furnishings of their house and the style of their clothes, and whole families that put on smiling faces with their Sunday clothes for a few hours at church.

The late A.W. Tozer commented on this situation in his book *Of God and Men*.

"Evangelicalism as we know it today... does produce some real Christians... but the spiritual climate into which many modern Christians are born does not make for vigorous spiritual growth. Indeed, the whole evangelical world is to a large extent unfavorable to healthy Christianity. And I am not thinking of modernism either. I mean rather the Bible-believing crowd that bears the name of orthodoxy....

"We are making converts to an effete type of Christianity that bears little resemblance to that of the New Testament. The average so-called Bible Christian in our times is but a wretched parody of true sainthood. Yet we put millions of dollars behind movements to perpetuate this degenerate form of religion, and attack the man who dares challenge the wisdom of it."

Everywhere I go I find young people who are aware of this split of Christian and secular values. Many have become atheists or agnostics because of it, while others have skidded into pits of indifference. Many Christians — leaders included — have admitted to me that their beliefs do not control their everyday lives.

Yet many are hungry for reality and genuineness in the Christian life. I met a student in an evangelical seminary who was first in his class academically, president of the campus mission group, and chaplain of the student body. In talking with me, he admitted that he had very little heart-knowledge of God, but he longed for a satisfying Christian experience.

Can this dichotomy be ended, this schizophrenia cured? Can Christ really revolutionize your life so it is consistent and productive? The answer is yes. I do not offer a formula to achieve this result, but I can offer the real Christ. I have seen Him revolutionize people's lives all over the world.

These Christians once lived in spiritual barrenness, then they honestly faced Christ and confessed their besetting sins that clung from the old life. Jesus transformed them, and He can transform you. It is not a life of perfection, but it is a life of reality. It does not mean a life of ease, but it is a life of joy.

If you're tired of split-level living, ask Jesus to make you a whole person.

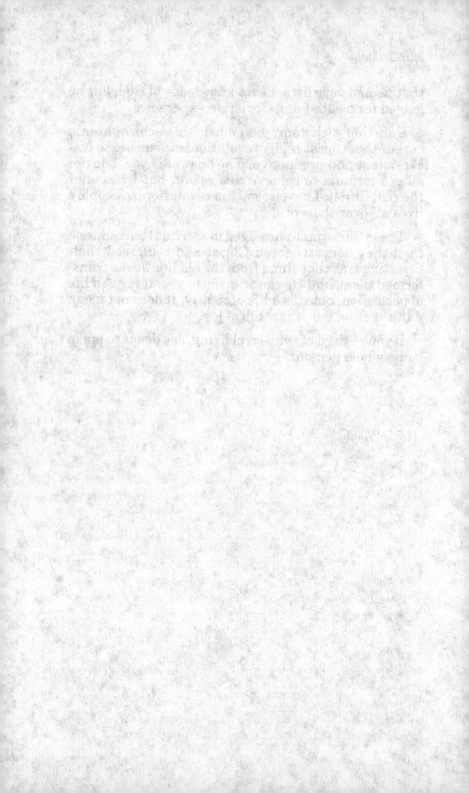

1

We Are Revolutionaries!

The Lord Jesus Christ was a revolutionary! Consider, if you will, some of His most basic teachings: "Love your enemies"; "Do good to them which hate you"; "Bless them which persecute you"; "Whosoever will be chief among you, let him be your servant"; "Lay not up for yourselves treasures on earth"; "Except a man forsake all that he hath, he cannot be my disciple."

Do you suppose that all these ideas fell in with the cultural pattern of Christ's day? Of course not! The people of his day were just as enslaved by the material aspect of living as the people of the twentieth century. But the Lord Jesus broke with any cultural pattern which interfered with the life of sacrificial love which He came to give!

In the history of Christianity there have been comparatively few who have lived according to the literal teachings of Christ. The early apostles did, of course. And the results for them were suffering, persecution, imprisonment, exile and death! Does this seem strange? No! These are the normal results of any life based upon the principles set forth by Christ.

Why is this? The answer is simple: the individual who would live this life is of necessity a revolutionary individual, a cultural nonconformist, a "fanatic," if you please! Literal adherence to the principles laid down by Jesus Christ would, without a doubt, result in worldwide revolution — a revolution motivated by love, a revolution executed by love, and a revolution culminating in love!

And we *are* revolutionaries! We are only a small group of Christian young people in Operation Mobilization, yet we have determined by God's grace to live our lives according to the revolutionary teachings of our Master. Within the sphere of absolute, literal obedience to his commands lies the power that will evangelize the world. Outside this sphere is the nauseating, insipid Christianity of our day.

We have committed ourselves in reckless abandonment to the claims of Christ on our blood-bought lives. We have no rights! Every petty, personal desire must be subordinated to the supreme task of reaching the world for Christ. We are debtors. We must not allow ourselves to be swept into the soul-binding curse of modern day materialistic thinking and living. Christians have been "willing" long enough to forsake all — the time has come (and is passing) when we must forsake all! Christ must have absolute control of our time and money. We must yield possessions, comforts, food and sleep; we must live on the barest essentials, that his cause might be furthered. The propagation of the faith we hold supreme! Christ is worthy of our all! We must be ready to suffer for Him and count it joy, to die for Him and count it gain. In the light of the present spiritual warfare, anything less than absolute dedication must be considered insubordination to our Master and mockery of His cause.

This is our commitment, and we will press forward until every person has heard the gospel. We will soon be in many different countries, engaged in combat with all the forces of darkness. We look beyond the thousands to the millions; beyond the cities to the countries. The world is our goal! And our primary targets are the seemingly impenetrable areas of the Communist and Moslem countries which can only receive freedom as they have opportunity to receive the Truth. These countries will be reached for Christ no matter what the cost. The ultimate victory is ours!

We must say to you, fellow Christian, that we are risen with Christ; we seek those things which are above, where Christ sits on the right hand of God. We have set our affections on things above, not on things on the earth, for we are dead and our life is hid with Christ in God. What blessed hope! What compelling truth to lead us to total abandonment of self and unto Christ! Without this, there is certain victory for the enemy and disgrace to our Lord Jesus Christ, who gave Himself for us that He might be all things to us!

(This manifesto for world evangelism, with minor changes here, was drawn up by twenty-five students in 1961, the beginning of Operation Mobilization, which the author now coordinates).

2

Hungry Disciples

Anyone who claims to be a disciple of Jesus Christ should be experiencing the reality of 1 John 2:6 — "He that saith he abideth in him (Christ) ought himself also to walk even as he walked." Without question, it is God's will for Christian disciples to live as Christ lived. This is not dry theory or a casual observation about Christian living; it is the dynamic standard which produces a vital witness for Christ to lost men and women.

Sometimes the men of the world are wiser in human affairs than the men of God. The agnostic H.G. Wells said in his *Outline of History*: "Not long after Jesus Christ died, those who claimed to follow Him gave up practicing His revolutionary principles." Yes, "revolutionary" was his description, and how right he was! The church has held on to structures and many of the doctrines, but it has lost the core of truth that Jesus taught.

Today you can meet more and more "say-evangelicals" as distinct from "be-evangelicals." As I have visited Bible school after Bible school and Christian institution after Christian institution, I found many "talkers" of Christianity - but few *walkers!* Not only I, but many Christian young people are acutely aware of this discrepancy. Many have been disillusioned by this contradiction between faith and life.

If we are informed, we realize that many of the young people who grow up in evangelical churches deny the faith before they are twenty-five. We wonder why, and some say, "It must be the latter days" — the days of apostasy and doom. That may be true, but that would not be sufficient explanation of our tragic losses to Satan.

Some Christians say the answer is in "good, sound, Bible teaching." But that is not enough, either. Never in the history of the Church have there been so many Bible conferences, radio Bible studies, and Bible study books. Did you know there are more than a thousand books available in the English language on the Pauline epistles? And today we have excellent recorded Bible studies as well. You can hear outstanding Bible teachers in your home by the turn of a radio knob.

We have every opportunity for learning of the life and teachings of Paul, but where are the Pauls of the twentieth century? Where are the men prepared like him and his companions to face cold and shipwreck and robbers for the gospel's sake, and to thank God for the stripes that tore their backs? We have many sincere servants of God and many great preachers. But where are those who can say with Paul that he ceased not to warn men and women night and day with tears? Such men are difficult to find, if not impossible. Why? The reason, I believe, is that we have separated our Bible beliefs from our daily living. Paul never did this.

We want to serve the Lord, and we say, "I am ready to serve the Lord if only I can find my place in His service!" Not finding it, we are frustrated. What is wrong?

God is far more concerned about your finding your place in Christ Himself than your place in His service. The essential thing in Christian living is not where you are going or what you are doing, but in whose strength you are living. You may go into Russia or just across the street to serve the Lord, *but in whose strength are you going?* Let us see how the Apostle Paul went about it. In Acts 20:19 we read of his

> "Serving the Lord with all humility of mind, and with many tears, and temptations (trials) which befell me by the lying in wait of the Jews. I kept back nothing that was profitable unto you, but have showed you, and have taught you publicly, and from house to house."

Notice the words: with all humility of mind." The apostle does not say he is serving the Lord with great preaching, literature distribution, tremendous campaigns in Russia or China, and great exploits in Turkey and India. He says that he served the Lord with many tears and trials. Discipleship is first of all a matter of the heart. Unless the heart is right, everything else is wrong. Our hearts need to experience a deep hunger and longing for God.

Hunger for God is the genuine mark of a disciple. It confirms to me that I am His child and that He is working in me. What I *do* for God does not prove that I am a disciple. I may try to fulfill the terms of the Sermon on the Mount or of church creeds; I may live ruggedly and sleep on the floor; but these things do not mark me as a disciple. The way I may know I am a disciple is my having an intense, insatiable hunger for the crucified Lord of Glory. If this is your experience—if you yearn for deep fellowship with your Creator, if you desire to know Him intimately and to walk with Him and to breathe with Him — though you may look like a failure and have made innumerable blunders, then you are well on the road to discipleship.

David was an Old Testament individual who knew God and walked with Him. Did God say: "David was a man who lived in purity all the days of his life"? No, God said that David was "a man after my own heart."

As we see in the Psalms, David had a hunger for God. "My heart longeth, yea, fainteth for the living God." "As the hart panteth after the water brooks, so panteth my soul after thee, O God." Despite David's failures and backsliding, he was hungry and thirsty for God. In church history right back to the beginning, we find that the mark of a true disciple, a man of God, is a hunger to know God and His righteousness.

The man after God's heart is described in Psalm 34. He can praise God for all his experiences.

> "I will bless the Lord at all times! His praise shall continually be in my mouth. My soul shall make her boast in the Lord: the humble shall hear thereof and be glad. Oh, magnify the Lord with me, and let us exalt his name together. I sought the Lord, and he heard me, and delivered me from all my fears" (verses 1-4).

And verse 10:

> "The young lions do lack, and suffer hunger; but they that seek the Lord shall not want any good thing."

They that seek the Lord: to seek and hunger for Him; to praise him continually; these are the marks of a true disciple of Jesus Christ.

Outward marks are often deceptive. The clever Christian, the one who excels in fluent praying or vigorous preaching, or the one who can answer all the theological questions, is not necessarily a disciple. Nor is it necessarily the one who has sold everything, down to the last shirt, in the act of "true discipleship". These things of themselves do not draw us close to God. But God draws near, the Scripture says, *"unto them that are of a broken heart, and saveth them that are of a contrite spirit."* No discovery of Christian truth has brought more encouragement to me than this one.

Do you remember Jesus' parable of the two men who came to the temple to pray? The first one went to the front and, surveying his audience, exulted, "O God, how thankful I am that I am not like that other man!" He may have remembered the rich man who turned away from Jesus because he had too many possessions, and then prayed: "God, I thank you that I am not like him, either. No Pharisee would do that!" Perhaps he thought of a young fellow who had never gone on a Pharisee Crusade, inspiring him to declaim: "Thank God I am not like that!" And then he unrolled a beautiful prayer that he learned in the Pharisee Bible College and arranged himself gracefully round the microphone to pray it to his public. But the second fellow, away off in the distance, bent over abjectly and beat his breast in agony, imploring: "God, have mercy on me."

To whom did God draw near? To the theological discourser, tossing out weightless words? Certainly not! As he strode off in his robes of self-righteousness, he knew nothing of God's justification or blessing.

God drew near to the one who came with a broken heart and contrite spirit. He heard the cry: "God, you know I am a failure. You know I am a phony. You know that I am worthless. I am a sinner! Have mercy on me." That man acknowledged his sins, and God justified him. This conflicts with our human understanding, yet it is one reason why I believe the Bible: no man would originate this way of salvation. This shows us the heart of God.

Except for Christianity, every religion offers a combination of service and reward: Do this and you will get that. So the average person would reason that if you are a good disciple of Jesus and live according to the Sermon on the Mount, or if you join evangelistic campaigns and hand out tracts, or perhaps if you shine the shoes of some person to prove how humble you are, then you will be rewarded with great blessing. But blessing comes only by God's way, not man's.

You, by yourself, can never shine anyone's shoes without false motives. You will not even distribute tracts without some personal ambition. Paul asked the Galatians: "Having begun in the Spirit, will you now continue in the flesh?" Many Christians are trying to do that. "I am saved by grace," they might say, "but now I must work my way through the Christian life."

This is a serious mistake. You are saved by God's grace, and by his grace you must serve. The Lord is near — not to the successful but to those who are of a broken heart. He saves — not the energetic but those who have a contrite spirit.

"Delight yourself in the Lord," says the psalmist, "and he will give you the desires of your heart," (Psalm 37:4). The reason we often fail to find the will of God is that we delight in other things. Christians engaged in evangelism are tempted to delight in the adventure of it. Or we delight in the fellowship of the gospel and the enthusiasm we share. I assure you that if you delight in any work for God or in any organization or movement, discouragement will sooner or later catch up with you. Our God is a jealous God, and he will not share his glory with an organization or a personality or a movement, however spiritual.

This is so clear in John 5:44, when Jesus says to disbelieving Jews: "How can you believe, which receive honor one of another, and seek not the honor that comes from God alone?" How can you believe God for great things — for laborers, for finances, for conversions, for victories in the lives of Christians — when you seek honor from other humans?

While we seek honor for ourselves, or try to advance the program or reputation of a movement or a preacher, we are building on the fragile merit of men. As the mark of a true disciple is his hunger for God, his goal is God's approval. When the work is done, he wants to hear God say, "Well done, thou good and faithful servant." Day after day he lives for God and His glory, seeking it as the deer craves the water of the brook.

Despite the weaknesses of Christ's people, there are many today who are hungry for God. This hunger must be cultivated both by feeding and by developing its capacity. God wants all of our being, not just our labor for the Lord, or our problem-solving, or our serving behind the scenes. We can get so caught up in activities, even Christian ones, that we lose conscious contact with God himself. He waits, close but silent, ready to remind us: "My child, you are too busy to receive strength from me."

His counsel remains: "Be still, and know that I am God" (Psalm 46:10). The only way to find the necessary power and resources for each day is to quietly wait on God. Plan for time to be alone with Him; learn to delight in Him; cultivate a hunger for His infinite being. Without this, your work will be superficial; with it, your deepest desires will be filled and your discipleship will glorify Him.

Our situation today is described well in these words by A.W. Tozer:

> "In this hour of all but universal darkness, one cheering gleam appears — within the fold of conservative Christianity there are to be found increasing numbers of persons whose religious lives are marked by a growing hunger after God himself. They are eager for spiritual realities, and will not be put off with words, nor will they be content with correct interpretations of the truth. They are athirst for God, and will not be satisfied until they have drunk deep at the Fountain of Living Water."

Many things have blinded our eyes; a multitude of theological distinctions and religious traditions have made a dichotomy between the doctrines of God and an intimate relationship with him. But there is hope wherever Christians are hungering for God. They are joined in a crusade to know God. This is the only cause that ultimately counts, the only link that will not be bent and broken by the ignorance and selfishness of men. Our real link is not with any organization, but with the living God. As we humble ourselves at the cross, we shall learn the reality of Jesus' power that conquered sin and death. We will receive the promise: *"Blessed are they who hunger and thirst after righteousness, for they shall be filled"* (Matthew 5:6).

3

ThePrayer of Freedom

"Litany" is a word that describes a formal prayer read by church people the same way each time. A great deal of litany was abandoned by the Protestant churches after the Reformation, and almost everything of Roman Catholic origin was rejected by the new churches. This resulted in some spiritual losses that we couldn't really afford, because some of the devout Roman Catholics can teach us vital truths. The power of the gospel and the presence of the Lord Jesus Christ infiltrate even somnolent churches, and some people come to know him and love him just as Martin Luther did within the Roman Church. If we Protestants possessed some of the spiritual depth evidenced by men such as Francis of Assisi, I believe we would accomplish far more for the Lord.

I do not know the name of the Roman Catholic who wrote the following litany, but it speaks of a life that all disciples of Christianity need to experience.

"O Jesus, meek and humble of heart, hear me.
Deliver me, Jesus,
from the desire of being loved,
from the desire of being extolled,
from the desire of being honored,

from the desire of being praised,
from the desire of being preferred to others,
from the desire of being consulted,
from the desire of being approved,
from the fear of being humiliated,
from the fear of being despised,
from the fear of suffering rebuke,
from the fear of being forgotten,
from the fear of being wronged,
from the fear of being suspected.

And, Jesus, grant me the grace to desire
that others might be loved more than I,
that others may be esteemed more than I,
that in the opinion of the world others may increase and I may decrease,
that others may be chosen, and I set aside,
that others may be praised and I unnoticed,
that others may be preferred to me in everything,
that others may become holier than I, provided that I become as holy as I should."

If we sincerely prayed like this every day, I am sure the Holy Spirit would marvelously change our lives. I believe the qualities spoken of in this prayer can become ours today. This should be our goal, not the accomplishment of any particular task for God.

There are many cheap substitutes and secondary roads for genuine holiness. We can tramp down one false route after another clutching the counterfeit of New Testament discipleship instead of possessing the real thing.

When I was a student, I was hungry to know what Christian holiness was, and I searched the Scriptures to find out the heart of the New Testament message. I came to the profound conviction that the Holy Spirit wants to produce Christlike individuals — not religious robots, not doctrinal champions, not evangelistic whirlwinds, but men who are like Jesus Christ. That is basically what this prayer is about.

These attributes are characteristics of Jesus. He was the one who was not esteemed, who was unloved, who was unextolled. He would not accept honor nor any of the things that ambitious men crave. He was the one who finally was completely despised and consequently executed. This prayer was written by a person who knew God intimately.

The work that God wants to do supremely in our hearts is to produce Christlikeness. It is a work that will take all our lives — there are no shortcuts to this kind of spiritual growth. There is no organization, no activity that can substitute for it. We need a constant hunger and thirst for the nature of Christ to be reproduced in us. We need, too, an awareness of the unending spiritual warfare surrounding us.

Men at war have to be ready to die any day. They may not know Christ, but they are ready to lose their lives as they go out to fight, or they are poor soldiers. We need something of the same spirit in spiritual warfare. We who have Christ's eternal life need to throw away our own lives. This readiness can come as we pray and live in the direction of this prayer.

It begins, ***"Deliver me, Jesus, from the desire of being esteemed."*** We all have an innate desire to be esteemed. However undistinguished we are, we like to be recognized. When we meet a new group of Christians and someone says, "Good to have you with us, brother! Would you like to share what God is doing in your life?" we feel gratified. But if we are ignored or slighted, we feel hurt. Whether we are extroverted or introverted, we selfishly desire attention, and so we all need to pray: "Lord, deliver me from the desire of being esteemed." In Philippians Paul warns against the product of inordinate self-esteem: "Let nothing be done through strife or vainglory, but in lowliness of mind let each esteem the other better than himself" (2:3). This requires the love-power of Jesus Christ.

The second petition of the prayer asks: ***"Deliver me, Jesus, from the desire of being loved."*** To be loved is our basic psychological need. Children cannot develop normally without love, and adults cannot function happily without the security of love. God met these needs supremely by giving His Son in love for us. "Hereby perceive we the love of God, because He laid down His life for us" (1 John 3:16). The greatest way God could demonstrate His love was to give His beloved, perfect Son to redeem us from sin. And His desire for us is that we should minister that same love to one another, for the same Scripture continues: "We ought to lay down our lives for the brethren.

I believe that some Christians strive anxiously for manifestations of God's love because we do not experience the love of fellow Christians which Christ commanded to be given. When there is little love flowing between us, we may feel impelled to seek special favors and blessings from God as confirmation that we are loved.

God's plan, according to the Scriptures, is for Christians to love one another, even as Christ loved the Church and gave Himself for it. The revolution of love is caught and passed on horizontally as well as vertically.

Most men who are on fire for God caught the spark from another man on fire. Great men of God grew to be like Christ because they had been with a man of God as well as with God Himself in communion. God meets us in prayer and in His Word, but He also meets us through the person and example of another brother.

I owe more than I can tell to the love and encouragement of other Christians. One of them is Billy Graham, though I do not know him personally. I have read his life story and followed his progress, and once I shook his hand in a crowd, and I felt his love even there.

I had gone to his office in London on business, and many people were there ahead of me. The whole office force was caught up in the pace of an evangelistic crusade, and nobody had spoken to my friend and me except the receptionist. Then Graham came in and immediately started shaking hands with everybody. He came straight to us and greeted us, and said something very kind. Here is a famous man who is fifty times busier than most people, but he had time to shake hands with the nobodies in his outer office. This was especially heartening to me, because I had found Christ as my Savior through Graham's preaching.

People will come to know Jesus if we go where they are and love them in this way, but the revolution of love cannot spread if we are intent on gaining love from others. We all need love, but the Christian disciple concentrates on giving love because he has received abundant love from God. A severe test comes when we feel unloved and rejected, as Jesus was. But at that crisis we may prove how wonderful the Lord's love is by giving ourselves for others.

The next snare we must be delivered from is ***"the desire of being extolled."*** I define "extol" as flattering or praising. How much we enjoy this! It is almost like feasting at a banquet. Jesus, we are told in Philippians, was just the opposite. He was "everything" in heaven, and he became as a criminal on earth. The Bible says: "Except a grain of wheat fall into the ground and die, it abideth alone." In order to be fruitful, the disciple must die to himself. Do not seek to be lifted up; be submerged.

This may be practiced every time we are overlooked or not given credit for our deeds. It is hard on the ego — which is just what the ego needs. This prayer helps to cut us off from the cancerous craving to be somebody, to gain a status superior to others. It checks the treacherous invasion of Satan among Christian workers.

Very close to this is the next plea: ***"Deliver me, from the desire of being honored."*** God said: "How can you believe which receive honor one of another, and seek not the honor that cometh from God only?" (John 5:44) Jesus' testimony was: "I receive not honor from men." Often when a Christian has accomplished something for God, he is tempted to exploit it for heightened personal honor. This temptation is from Satan. Some honors and recognitions are very subtly harmful. They come from well-intentioned people or Christian organizations, and the commendations become food for self-exaltation. Sometimes we can receive more honor from fellow Christians than from the world system, and the "sanctified" source makes the praise all the more insidious.

There is even a danger of our seeking spiritual experiences for self-aggrandizement. We are tempted to testify of deliverance from sin, or answered prayer, or some other experience of God's grace in a way that brings vast satisfaction to ourselves rather than honor to God. His grace is to be prized, but it is not to be flaunted as a sign of our merit.

I sometimes get letters from young people seeking training, who write recommending themselves. They tell me how great they are, and how many qualifications they have. Can you imagine getting a letter like that from the Apostle John? There was of course a time when, like the others, John sought credit and even precedence for having followed Jesus, but that was before the cross brought about a revolution in all their lives. It is not wrong to be encouraged. What is wrong is the seeking of praise and commendation from others. Do we praise God as much when we are alone as when we're with others? Do we continue our work alone with as much enthusiasm as we did when we were being observed? I dislike working alone and believe in working two by two. But sometimes we are alone, and then we are tested as to whether we are concerned for our honor or for God's.

The next prayer is very close in meaning: ***"Deliver me from the desire of being praised."*** This is related to everyday associations and deeds. If we are hungry for praise, we eagerly accept crumbs of approval from anyone, whether they are sincere and honest or not. Such praise turns rotten on the tongue of fickle and unprincipled men.

We also pray: ***"Deliver me from the desire of being preferred to others."*** How do we feel when we are qualified and someone else is chosen? Do we rejoice when a fellow Christian receives honor? This blessing to another may cut us deeply. A.W. Tozer said, "The cross will cut into our lives where it hurts the worst, sparing neither us nor our carefully cultivated reputations." Worldly men put great stock in their ranking, but John the Baptist easily declared: "He that cometh after me is preferred before me."

"Deliver me, too, from the desire of being consulted." Our experience and knowledge are hindrances when we expect others to defer to us and acknowledge our wisdom. Being overlooked is especially trying when our advice seems to be so obviously right. But this is another form of self-serving, as we can trust God to employ our advice if it is needed for His glory.

Most of us need deliverance also from ***"the desire of being approved"*** — of being assured by others that we were right, after all. Disciples must continue to be learners in God's school of life. When people ask me what degree I am studying for, I reply "The A.U.G. — Approved Unto God." It will not be awarded in this life, but it is the only one that matters eternally.

A common burden we carry is ***"the fear of being humiliated."*** We want to "look good" to others, even desiring to make favorable impressions "for God." But God does not have this problem —in His perfection and power, He is never humbled. And His Son did not shrink from the humiliations of men when He was on earth.

God often takes us the same way His Son went. The humiliations dramatize the contrast between God's ways and man's, and point the way to safety. Records show that swimmers who have practiced life-saving are vulnerable to drowning because they are overconfident in the water. God would save us from overconfidence in self, and so He humbles us. He undermines and weakens our naturally strong points for our good and our growth in Him. Let us not fear the humiliation that can bring this valuable benefit.

Deliver us too, Lord, from ***"the fear of being despised."*** Oh, how we need this fearlessness for witnessing. So many people scorn the Christian who witnesses for Christ. The distributor of tracts may be despised, but we who know their value should give them out as though they were bank notes. Some people resent the "invasion of their privacy" concerning spiritual matters, but the Christian witness is investing in eternity. May God's love fully cast out this fear.

The ***"fear of suffering rebuke"*** clutches at most Christians, yet we need correction to avoid lagging in our discipleship. Christians must learn to speak to one another both in love and rebuke. Though we learn primarily from the Spirit of God, He may use a brother or sister to teach us. Earnest disciples can expect God to speak through His Word, through prayer, and through the exhortations of a brother.

God has given me, I believe, increasing grace to take rebukes, but it has taken years. I reacted like a rattlesnake to the first rebukes I got as a Christian. There's a great difference between a rattlesnake and a worm. The Bible compares Jesus to a worm in the treatment He received (Psalm 22:6). If you strike a worm, it wriggles or dies, but if you strike a rattlesnake, you are struck in return. How significant it is that Satan is described as a serpent!

Our twenty-five reasons why the other fellow is wrong and we are right are always near the tip of our tongue. But our readiness or reluctance to defend ourselves is a measure of our spirituality. Let us implore God to make us unafraid to receive rebukes.

Then there is the almost universal ***"fear of being forgotten."*** In India, where living conditions are so poor, some people hoard money to make sure a beautiful memorial over their grave will remind the living of their name. Some Christian churches also are filled with memorials that perpetuate the names and prestige of the dead.

Most of us fear being forgotten by friends. If we don't struggle to prove our worthiness or helpfulness, our past contributions may be forgotten — and us too.

But life is not lived in the past. Service, satisfaction, and sharing are experienced in the present. Forgetting the things that are past — though we can never forget the people — we press on for today's goal. Let us fear being remembered only for the past. God remembers every good thing we do, and that's sufficient.

"Deliver me, Jesus, from the fear of being ridiculed." Wise is the person who can laugh at himself! Sometimes there is such good cause! Sometimes the ridicule is malicious and is intended to hurt. It may be difficult to realize at such times that the ridicule is a boomerang, injuring the source. The Bible says: "The Lord looks on the heart," and if my heart is right I may be filled with peace. As we bare our hearts to Him, He is quick to reassure when man is quick to ridicule.

"The fear of being wronged" may keep us from trusting people. This fear can be crippling, preventing us from taking a step of faith immediately before us.

The closely related ***"fear of being suspected"*** immobilizes some Christians. But we are always going to be misunderstood by someone, no matter what we do. Praying often in meetings will cause some to think you are trying to display your spirituality. We cannot afford to be bound by fear of what others may think. "Rejoice," said Jesus, "when men shall say all manner of evil against you falsely for my sake." We can come to that place of liberty where, because we love the Lord

Jesus and act in faith, we are not anxious about what other people think or suspect.

The second section of this prayer deals with worthy desires. ***"Jesus, grant me the grace to desire that others be loved more than I."*** This reminds us of the need people have for love which I can help to supply. Wherever I go I meet people who need love and attention — to be visited, listened to, written to, prayed with. How can this enormous need be met? Only by God's grace working in me that others may be esteemed more than I.

"Grant me the desire that in the opinion of the world others may increase, and I may decrease." The testimony of John the Baptist is unequivocal: "I must decrease." The following phrases of the prayer: ***"That others may be chosen, and I set aside; that others may be preferred to me in everything; that others may be praised and I unnoticed"*** are summed up in this principle that Jesus Christ must increase, but I must decrease. I must hide behind the cross, that my Lord may be seen and worshipped. I must recognize myself as nobody, so Jesus will be my All.

The final clause is revolutionary: ***"That others may become holier than I, provided that I become as holy as I should."*** There is always a danger that Christians may have such a hunger for spiritual reality that we tread on other people in our search for it. The Christian life is not a competition with others; we have a common goal and we grow together in the strength and grace of the body of believers. We must drink together at the Fountain of Living Water.

Can we honestly pray this amazing prayer? I am reminded of some words of A.W. Tozer that I have written in the front of my Bible:

> "The Church at this moment needs men who feel themselves expendable in the warfare of the soul. Such men will be free from the compulsions that control weaker men, the lust of the eyes, the lust

> of the flesh, and the pride of life. They will not be forced to do things by the squeeze of circumstances. Their only compulsion will come from within and from above. This kind of freedom is necessary if we are going to have prophets in our pulpits again instead of mascots. These free men will serve God and men from motives too high to be understood by the rank and file who today shuffle in and out of the sanctuary. They will make no decision out of fear, they will take no course out of a desire to please, accept no service for financial consideration. They will perform no religious act out of mere custom. Nor will they allow themselves to be influenced by the love of publicity, or by the desire for reputation."

The link between this passage and the prayer is clearly etched. It is as though these two spokesmen, the earlier Catholic and the modern evangelical, learned in the same school. And they have, for they both studied at the feet of Jesus.

4

The Land of Rest

If the Promised Land was a country to conquer under the leadership of Joshua, it was also a place of rest and victory for the Israelites. A "Promised Land" also awaits the Christian who is willing to move from the wilderness wanderings of self-effort and frustration.

> "Let us therefore fear, lest, a promise being left us of entering into his rest, any of you should seem to come short of it. For unto us was the gospel preached, as well as unto them: but the word preached did not profit them, not being mixed with faith in them that heard it. For we which have believed do enter into rest, as He said, As I have sworn in my wrath, if they shall enter into my rest: although the works were finished from the foundation of the world. For He spake in a certain place of the seventh day in this wise. And God did rest the seventh day from all His works.
>
> "And in this place again, if they shall enter into my rest. Seeing therefore it remaineth that some must enter therein, and they to whom it was first preached entered not in because of unbelief: Again, He limiteth a certain day, saying in David, today, after so long a time; as it is said, today if

> ye will hear His voice, harden not your hearts. For if Jesus had given them rest, then would He not afterward have spoken of another day. There remaineth therefore a rest to the people of God. For he that is entered into His rest, he also hath ceased from his own works, as God did from His. Let us labor therefore to enter into that rest, lest any man fall after the same example of unbelief"
> (Hebrews 4:1-11).

So many Christians are carrying burdens. Though we try to drop them or run away from them, they cling like mud on our feet and fear on our mind. These burdens are carryovers from our pre-Christian days, and God intends Christians to be rid of them.

The account of Israel's coming out of Egypt and entering the Promised Land, Canaan, is a graphic picture of the full redemption we have in Jesus Christ. It vividly describes God's intervention into human affairs as well as the variety and complexity of problems encountered by God's people. Paul reminds us that "these things were written for our example."

Moses, the man who received from God the Ten Commandments, inscribed on stone, did not understand God's ways in his earlier years. He did forsake prestige and privilege in the Egyptian hierarchy to identify himself with God's people, but he recklessly asserted himself on behalf of the Israelites instead of acting by God's direction. The result was a forty year exile in the Sinai wilderness. There, from a burning bush, God called and commissioned Moses to return to Egypt and deliver Israel.

Moses was afraid, so keenly was he aware of his past failure. When God told him to go, he said, "They won't listen to me." He pleaded, "I can't speak...." Moses was like so many ambassadors of God who have begun with: "I'll never be a witness for Christ; I can hardly speak. I'll never be a missionary; I don't like spiders and snakes; I can't sleep on the floor. I'll never do this because I am afraid of that." Yet God did such stupendous things through Moses.

Israel's exit from slavery in Egypt is a picture of the Christian's deliverance from sin's bondage. God's judgment fell on the unrepentant Egyptians but not upon the people who were marked by the blood of the Passover lamb. After the angel of death struck Egyptian homes, Pharaoh capitulated and ordered: "Let them go," and the nation of slaves started for the Promised Land.

They had not gone far before Pharaoh changed his mind and started after them. If Moses thought his troubles were over after getting out of Egypt, his education was just beginning.

Leading one of the largest mobilization operations in history, Moses was doing quite well shepherding a million people and innumerable animals toward the open spaces and safety. Then billowing dust from the fast-moving war chariots of Egypt signaled the pursuit of a vengeful army, and fear swept through the refugees. "Moses," they cried, "you've brought us out here to be killed. Why didn't you let us stay back there? Things in Egypt weren't that bad!"

Hedged in by grumbling people, advancing Egyptian solders bent on slaughtering or recapturing them, and rolling waves that blocked their flight, Moses appeared in a desperate strait. But the appearance was deceiving.

Moses cried to God for help, and then obeyed God's command to wait for deliverance. Another miracle took place as the waters of the Red Sea parted and the wind made a dry path for the Israelites to walk over. They hurried across, hardly able to believe their eyes, and the chariots of Pharaoh raced to overtake them. All at once the waters swept back, and chariots, Egyptians, and Pharaoh were gone!

Satan is not finished when Christ first delivers us from his clutches. The night I was converted, I stepped out of Madison Square Garden in New York where I had accepted Christ, and bumped into solid opposition. It was in the form of a belligerent youth anxious to demonstrate his masculinity. I objected to a crude remark made about girls, and this street pugilist deposited me on the concrete with one blow. That was my introduction to the Christian life — I learned early that it's a warfare!

The problems Moses faced in the wilderness were problems every Christian leader has. The people complained about the arrangements, questioned Moses' motives, and wistfully recalled the few pleasures they'd left behind. Somewhat like the twentieth-century Church, they whined, "Of course, we want to be free, but can't we take a little of Egypt with us? We don't want to live back there, but some Egyptian styles can't hurt!"

But God had promised them a place of rest, a land overflowing with milk and honey. He never intends His people to subsist indefinitely on manna rations. The wilderness crossing to Canaan was short, and they could have entered directly. But the advance scouts saw only hazards and enemies in the Promised Land. "There are giants over there," they stammered. "We are like insects in their eyes. We can never possess such a land." And they were immobilized by distrust of God.

Today we hear and see the same disbelief. "It cannot be done!" "There are giants in the land — Buddhism, Islam, Communism." "We must forget the countries closed to the gospel." Like Israel, the Church often does not see that the place of challenge is also the place of rest.

There were two "fools for Christ" in Israel: Caleb and Joshua. They were prepared to believe God and act, and they later entered the Promised Land. The great majority were doomed to wander, struggle, and die in the wilderness. How many men of faith and vision in our generation have pointed to the place of spiritual rest and gone unheeded? Still the Promised Land waits.

We cannot live a life of victory in the "wilderness" of unbelief and disobedience. If we go to serve the Lord in Asia or Europe or America — or wherever — and we go in doubt, burdened with problems and wrestling opposition in our own strength, we shall experience steady failure and discouragement.

Hebrews 4:10 declares that "he that is entered into His rest, he has ceased from his own works as God did from His." Any work for God that depends on our own efforts, our own zeal, our own ability, and resources, will fail. The place of victory and rest is the place of God's works, not ours. We are active and completely involved, but the victory does not depend on us and the cause for anxiety is gone.

We can enter into God's rest now because Christ has entered it for us. When we contemplate what Christ did for us on the cross, we realize that God has genuinely identified us with Christ. Through our faith in the One who died for us, we have been "crucified with Christ" — identified with Him in His death. If you are a Christian, you have been crucified with Christ! It is not something that can occur in the future if we trust enough, or pray effectively, or memorize another seventy-eight Scripture verses. No, we are to see ourselves dying to sin with Christ on His cross, and as the truth dawns we can find ourselves entering into His spiritual rest just as the people of Israel found the Jordan parted and their inheritance open to them as they crossed over. This entrance takes place when we recognize that Christ is our *All* — our strength, our guidance, our hope, our victory — and although the battle is not over, the anxiety and fear are.

Some people know the exact day on which they were born again. For me it happened on March 5, 1955. Others have just as real an experience, but cannot tell the date of it. They do know it happened. It is the same when we enter this experience of victory — we may not be able to explain it or tell when it happened, but we know that we are in a new relationship to God.

No man can offer truly effective service to the Lord unless he has entered this life of restful trust in God, this victory of the risen Christ. Because then, just as we are truly identified with Christ in His vanquishing of sin and death, so we are identified with Him in His risen life. We cease our struggle in self-centered accomplishments and live by the power of Jesus' resurrection. That is real victory.

This is the only way to success in Christian living. It is the way of faith, the same kind of faith that brought us salvation. "The just shall live *by faith*" (Romans 1:17). "As you have therefore received Christ Jesus the Lord, so walk in Him" (Colossians 2:6). Then we shall say with Paul, "I live, yet not I, but Christ liveth in me" (Galatians 2:20). When we have entered God's place of rest, we cease from our selfish strivings and the worries that accompany them.

There are times when I have a hundred letters on my desk, many of them about problems. Where should evangelism teams go? Where is the money to support them? How shall we find the vehicles to move teams and literature to their destination? I have learned from 1 Peter 5:7 what to do with them: "Casting all your care upon Him, for He careth for you." Sometimes I can say, "Lord, those letters, those telegrams are all yours. I'm going to bed."

Sleep is a wonderful blessing, and we must not let worry rob us of it. I do not believe in worry because I believe in God's place of rest. I believe that Jesus Christ was crucified for all the worries of the world, and if the Lord Jesus did that, then why should I be anxious about them? This applies to every area of life, every frustration, every inferiority feeling, everything that bothers me. All these things cannot defeat me unless I leave the place of rest — my security in Christ.

As Christians we know that we walk daily in a wilderness world, but the attractions of the wilderness need not walk in us. Whenever they intrude through our eyes or ears or mind, the citizen in the Promised

Land must pray: "Lord, I used to enjoy that diversion in slavery, but I have died to that in Christ; hold me in your rest and resurrection life." It is ours for the asking and the trusting.

The Promised Land of rest on this earth is not for sleeping; it is for fighting — but it is the place where you hear God say: "I shall fight for you." Opposition, danger, temptations and hardships surround you, but your spirit rests in the fortress of God's love and power. Will you choose this sanctuary instead of trying to straddle the Jordan and keep one foot in the world? It's the most important thing you can do in response to this book.

5

Front Line Perils

Have you decided to walk the road of discipleship? Are you determined to follow Christ wherever He leads? Then be prepared for obstructions, washouts, and falling rocks! For it is absolutely certain that you have a rough road ahead of you.

One of the ways God helps the disciple is to give a glimpse in Scripture of the perils encountered on the way to a victorious Christian life.

> "Moreover, brethren, I would not that ye should be ignorant, how that all our fathers were under the cloud, and all passed through the sea; and were all baptized unto Moses in the cloud and in the sea; and did all eat the same spiritual meat; and did all drink the same spiritual drink: for they drank of that spiritual Rock that followed them: and that Rock was Christ.
>
> "But with many of them God was not well pleased: for they were overthrown in the wilderness. Now these things were our examples, to the intent we should not lust after evil things, as they also lusted. Neither be ye idolaters, as were some of them; as it is written, the people sat down to eat and drink, and rose up to play. Neither let us

> commit fornication, as some of them committed, and fell in one day three and twenty thousand. Neither let us tempt Christ, as some of them also tempted, and were destroyed of serpents. Neither murmur ye, as some of them also murmured, and were destroyed of the destroyer.
>
> "Now all these things happened unto them for ensamples: and they are written for our admonition, upon whom the ends of the world are come. Wherefore let him that thinketh he standeth take heed lest he fall. There hath no temptation taken you but such as is common to man: but God is faithful, who will not suffer you to be tempted above that ye are able; but will with the temptation also make a way to escape that ye may be able to bear it" (1 Corinthians 10:1-13).

Notice particularly that Paul says these experiences are examples "for our admonition." He is warning about the many hazards that beset Christians. Although these Israelites shared in God's revelation of power to Moses in the pillar, cloud and the retreating sea, and though they received the same spiritual sustenance, they failed to pass the stern tests that Moses overcame. In a similar way, the Christian leaves Egypt — the world — and crosses the Red Sea — which speaks, I believe, of salvation. He begins to sing of his liberation, just as the Israelites did when they saw the Red Sea rolled back and the enemy wiped out behind them. But he fails to realize that mighty enemies are still ahead.

Ancient Simeon Stylites lived on top of a flag pole for thirty years, yet he did not escape trials. You may isolate yourself anywhere and still face conflicts. Why? Because the enemy roves within you. The people of Israel fled from the giants of Canaan, but suffered defeat after defeat in the deserted wilderness. Only Joshua and Caleb survived of the pioneer travelers, because they trusted in God.

These two men illustrate the reality of heart commitment to God. They could easily have differed with each other, but their hearts were right with God. Caleb, for example, said, "Let us go up at once, and occupy it; for we are well able to overcome it." Some observers might have accused him of self-confidence, but God knew his faithful intention. Joshua focused his words on God: "If the Lord delights in us, He will bring us into this land and give it to us."

What thrills me is that both men walked with God, both entered the Promised Land, and both were richly blessed. They did not judge the other's motives by a variation in terminology. And neither should we. A young Christian with wrong vocabulary and ill-expressed doctrine may actually be trusting in the work of Christ more than Mr. Deeper-Life who has it all turned out to the last syllable. Caleb's and Joshua's key to entry into Canaan was the same: their sincere, persevering response to God's promise.

I believe the land of Canaan speaks of the Christian's victorious life. The salvation of God has taken us across "Jordan," but most Christians languish on the border of the Promised Land. We stubbornly disbelieve the mountain ascent will bring us to our inheritance, and we hide among the rocks in the valley.

We must go on, though we are not entering a picnic ground or holiday camp when we cross Jordan. Battles, struggles, trials, and defeats are ahead in the Promised Land, but so are victory and joy and power. After truly entering this land, you will know more of God's fullness and power, thrilling answers to prayer, and intimacy of true discipleship. Yet you will be amazed that the battle can be so fierce. At times there may be no more than bare necessities supplied. Here we realize we are in a fight to the finish with sin, self, and Satan.

The realization that we are involved in a constant spiritual warfare can be a great source of strength and comfort. When some difficult situation arises or fiery darts from Satan pierce us, we realize that this is part of God's wonderful plan for us. My wife and I can testify that it is doing wonders for us in our married life. Friends often give advice: "You should do this..."; "All parents do that..."; but we are able to go on our knees and say, "That's right, Lord, in times of peace, but this is war!"

We are helped when we reflect on this century's two world wars. Think of the demands made upon young men; think of the anxieties suffered by wives and children. And we have been given the privilege of fighting in the battlefield alongside the Lord of glory, the Captain of our salvation. What sacrifice can be too great for Him? Compared with what Christ did on the cross for us, our service for God is nothing.

Someone has said, "the devil doesn't waste his fiery darts on nominal Christians." The history of war confirms that armies make opposing leaders their targets. Satan uses the same tactics. He does not waste time on those who are not counting for God; he aims for the active disciple. When the devil sees someone steadfastly following Christ, he goes into a strategy meeting with the demons of hell and together they plan a full-scale attack. If we understand something of the enemy's movements and are armed against them, we shall not be caught unawares.

Two tactics we are told to use against the devil are to resist and to run. I have always been a better "runner" than "resister," but I want to learn more about resisting in God's strength. The Word of God tells us to "flee" Satan's temptations (2 Timothy 2:22). It says to resist him, not in our own power, but in the power of the cross of Christ (James 4:7). The atoning blood of Jesus Christ removes the guilt of our sin, and the cross severs Satan's control over us. The crucified life of a disciple is maintained only as other camouflaged perils are recognized and avoided.

The first is pride. The Word of God says, "Pride goeth before destruction" (Proverbs 16:18). We need to ask God to search our hearts and root out this subtle peril that has time and again ruined Christian men. I have seen young men dedicated, zealous, filled with the Spirit, and seemingly being used by God, become totally ineffective because of pride. They have seen answers to prayer and are sure they are getting through to God. Or they have been greatly used by God in the salvation of souls. Or they have been told that they are exceptionally gifted in some way. Then spiritual conceit invades and takes over.

One mark of spiritual and emotional stability is to remain unaffected by commendation. Such a person can take the praise and honor of men realistically. He knows where the true honor is due.

The unstable person receives praise and clutches it protectively. If he is told he is weak in a particular area, he will nurse the memory of someone telling him this was his strong point! A balanced Christian knows how to accept the praise of men with diffidence and to welcome their criticism with concern. When you begin to accomplish something for God, watch for pride to follow and repent of it before the cross.

There is a kind of pride that elevates us while debasing others. We must be careful of criticizing Christians for not having attained something spiritual which we believe we have gained. But we have not gained it if we indeed do possess it; we have received it from God.

It helps me sometimes to think what I will be like forty years from now: will I preach with as much zeal, as much urgency, as much exercise of spirit as now? I can't know, and I must be careful what I say about others.

Someone has pointed out to me that the defects which we sometimes see and judge in others may be battle scars suffered in faithful service to Christ. Perhaps the Christian has seen more and harder battles than we. He may have won many battles, but not without scars and wounds in the process.

We might consider older men of God old-fashioned and short on zeal. Younger Christians must show mercy to the older generation, and I ask them in return to have mercy in their dealings with us. God wants both the older and younger generations to realize neither would be anything without Christ and his grace.

The kindred peril to pride is a critical spirit. It seems easy to see distinctly everything that is wrong with other people. But psychologists tell us that the things we most readily criticize in others are sometimes things which are wrong in our own lives. This is called projection, and some Christians unwittingly specialize in it.

When I tested myself on this, the results scared me. If, day in and day out, I was seeing something wrong in other people, was it really a reflection of some weakness in my own personality or habits? I saw others' inconsistencies so readily. One man tended to be superficial; another seemed to say things that he did not mean; a third was weak on economizing time. Could it be true that these weaknesses supposedly contrasted with my strengths, the comparison was neither fair nor kind.

Paul instructed Christians in Philippians 4 to think positively:

> "Finally, brethren, whatsoever things are true, whatsoever things are honest, whatsoever things are just, whatsoever things are pure, whatsoever things are lovely, whatsoever things are of good report, if there be any virtue and if there be any praise, think on these things."

I believe this represents part of the revolution in men's lives that Christ came to bring. It is a revolution that replaces complaint with wholesome and affirmative thinking, a revolution that passes over people's mistakes and follies to bring God's light and love on the scene.

One time I was running to catch a train in Stockholm and hot criticism welled up within me against the brother who had mixed up the schedule and got me to the station ten minutes after the train was due to leave. "Why cannot people who have lived in Stockholm all their lives read their timetables?" I thought to myself. I wanted to get to Gothenberg the next morning in order to investigate a ship that might serve our goal of world evangelism.

I left the station, battling with myself, until the Lord brought Romans 8:28 to my mind. Some might say that this verse is a "crutch" for the crippled, but I was feeling crippled as I sought victory over the feelings in my heart. I leaned on the promise: "All things work together for good to them that love God, to those who are the called according to His purpose." And in faith I was able to praise God that I did not catch the train.

That night the train I had missed crashed. I offer no explanation for the crash, but I learned to be more careful about concluding that disappointing events are mistakes. We make mistakes, but our God does not. And with infinite patience and foresight, he specializes in overruling ours.

The Bible tells us God has entrusted the treasures of the Holy Spirit to the clay pots of our bodies as containers. In our work for the Lord we often mess up His purpose. There are times when I could weep for marring the wonder of His truth with my corroded personality, my beat-up pot. But God's sovereign power overrules and makes the crudest, weakest, lowliest, most out-of-place testimony for him count for eternity.

If we have a greater vision of our God, our negativeness and criticism will diminish or vanish. When we fully realize that our human leaders are learners like the rest of us, we can concentrate on God and be delivered from a critical spirit.

Another peril to the victorious Christian is becoming accustomed to spiritual things. As we see the power of God at work, answering prayer and accomplishing the impossible in people's lives, we may find ourselves being callous about the miraculous.

A team working in Operation Mobilization met for prayer in Zaventem, Belgium, and quite a few stayed to pray until 3 a.m. The financial needs of the work were acute and God stirred us to a great exercise of faith. When we went to bed, we had a thrilling consciousness that God was going to work. The next morning I had to phone our central office in England for some other business. On the phone someone asked me if I had heard about the large gift which had come from another country. The telegram announcing the gift had come into our office that very day. The amount was some $6,000. The money did not come from someone who was stirred up in the prayer meeting, but from someone thousands of miles away, who had sent it sometime earlier. We have seen things like this happen for over a decade, and we simply praise God for His answers to prayer. But there is a grave danger of becoming familiar with the miraculous, casual about God moving in wonderful ways.

The Bible says that there is rejoicing in the presence of the angels over one soul that repents, but sometimes we do not rejoice unless it is a dozen. I remember at Bible College when I went out and was able to help someone find Christ. I really got excited and would barge into a fellow student's room bubbling with joy. "Come on, drop your work, let's have a prayer meeting, brother. Let's give up some time to praise the Lord." A week later, another brother would come to see me. He was not as loudmouthed as I: "Praise the Lord, George; a fellow down the street accepted Christ tonight." What was my reaction? "Oh, praise God; that's good. Amen." And back I went to my studies. May God forgive us for letting ourselves become over familiar with holy things, or rejoice over our victory and not over that of the other fellow.

Such familiarity can be heartbreaking in gatherings of God's people. Sometimes we meet around the Lord's Table to remember His death and there is less praise among us than if we shared a meal of ham and eggs after a long night. The Israelites in the wilderness took God's miracles for granted: they became accustomed to manna, and craved meat. God gave them the meat they desired, and leanness filled their souls. It can happen to us, too.

Another peril of the Christian life is asceticism. If we seek hardship because it builds our reputation, we are not suffering for Christ's sake. An example of this was a young man on a witnessing tour who was invited to stay overnight at a Christian home where the hostess went to a lot of trouble to prepare a comfortable bed. The young man stiffened proudly and announced that he no longer slept in beds. He had forgotten — or had never learned — that Paul knew how both to be abased and to abound. This balance is difficult, but it is possible as we make love our way and Christ our goal.

Asceticism is not nearly such a problem as its opposite — *laziness and the love of ease.* This is one of the most deadly perils for a Christian in the position of independent responsibility. Discipline is good for us, and laziness is a great sin. One reason the Church lacks foot soldiers is that it lacks people who want to work hard. Nehemiah's men finished their task because they had a "mind to work." When the pressures of duties relax, laziness becomes a tremendous danger to many Christians.

Then there is the serious peril of disqualification. When God begins to use you significantly, the devil closes in to discover some flaw that he can exploit and scandalize. Evangelist Alan Redpath has pointed out that King David's sin with Bathsheba was preceded by his sinful withdrawal from battle. While his troops were fighting the enemy, he was at leisure, and his relaxation physically and spiritually opened him to the whirlwind of temptation that swept him into sinful lust and God's judgment.

This illustrates the peril of being away from the place God has called us to, of breaking communion with the Lord Jesus Christ, of self-indulgence, and of arrogant criticism. These give Satan his chance to invade our spirit and inflame sin that will dishonor God and ruin our testimony. Though the sin can be forgiven, the consequences may hinder the gospel for years.

Perils still beset the Christian living in the Promised Land, and we must be aware of them. We must remember the warning in 1 Corinthians 10:12: "Let him that thinketh he standeth take heed lest he fall." God's provision for us amid the dangers is constant: "There hath no temptation taken you but such as is common to man; but God is faithful... He will make a way of escape" (10:13). Choose it, and God's grace will bring victory.

6

Love That Conquers

In John 13:34, 35 we read these words of Jesus : "A new commandment I give unto you, that you love one another; as I have loved you, that you also love one another. By this shall all men know that you are my disciples, if you have love one to another." This is the touchstone of Christianity and the dynamic of the revolution that was begun by Jesus Christ Himself.

Some Christians seem to have misread this verse. They apparently see : "By this shall all men know that you are my disciples, that you have no possessions." Or " ... that you read and carry your Bibles." Or perhaps "... that you have sound doctrine." Or maybe that "... you traverse land and sea to win converts to Christ."

But Jesus said none of those things. He said that there is one major thing that will convince the world we are His disciples, and that is the love we have for one another. We are not the disciples of a theory or doctrine or institution, but disciples of the loving Jesus! His love led Jesus to give His life for us, and that kind of love is commanded between Jesus' followers.

People sometimes ask me, "How do you conceive of the love of God?" My answer is found in 1 John 3:16: "In this we perceive the love of God, in that he laid down his life for us." As a consequence, says John: "So we ought to lay down our lives for the brethren." This is the supreme love, Jesus told us, for: "Greater love has no man than this, that a man lay down his life for his friends" (John 15:13).

Love is the essence of discipleship: it is the wall that surrounds a disciple, the roof that protects him, and the ground which supports him. The Bible says emphatically that though I speak with tongues of men and of angels, have all wisdom, make tremendous sacrifices, give my body to be burned, and relinquish all I own, I am worth nothing if I have not done them in love.

Most of us have to admit that we know very little about actually loving people. We know that we have often loved because of the benefits that come to us. Divine love is impartial; it loves the repulsive and the attractive, the beggar and the merchant prince.

Is this love really possible? And does it work? When I give myself for the sake of another, when I "fall into the ground and die" in order to bear fruit, when I deny myself and take up the cross and follow Jesus — does it make a revolutionary difference? Or would it turn me into a blind fanatic rushing from one good deed to another and getting trampled by the strong?

This love is possible, and it is very practical. It does not come naturally, nor does it come instantly in a rededication service or some particular experience. Real love comes from God, who is love, and it is developed in the hard school of life over many years. There may be a crisis for appropriating God's love, but a process of expressing love follows or it all becomes an abscess.

The Bible speaks clearly on how to acquire and develop God's love. The first thing it tells me is that love is a fruit of the Spirit (Galatians 5:22). As every Christian has the Spirit, every Christian may have this love. Ephesians 5:18 gives one of the few commands about the Holy Spirit in the New Testament: "Be not drunk with wine, wherein is excess; but be filled with the Spirit." The filling produces an overflow that touches other people.

What are evidences of the filling of the Spirit? "… Speaking to [among] yourselves in psalms and hymns and spiritual songs." This is joy and encouragement shared with other Christians. And it also communicates with God: "…singing and making melody in your hearts to the Lord; giving thanks always for all things." These signs accompany the love given by the Holy Spirit.

The Scriptures also teach that prayer will develop this love. Paul is our example: "I bow my knees unto the Father of our Lord Jesus Christ… that He would grant you… to be strengthened by His Spirit… and to know the love of Christ, which passeth knowledge" (Ephesians 3:14, 16, 19).

As the Lord blesses the person prayed for, He will also work in your heart. We are sometimes partly responsible for other's weaknesses, and weaknesses in a brother's life may reflect weaknesses in our own. If I have been spiritually discerning of something wrong, through prayer I can help to change it. Let us pray earnestly for the people we do not like or do not understand, and God will make changes in the situation. We have many examples of this in Scripture, and we are exhorted to pray for all men, even our enemies, said the Lord Jesus.

Another helpful step is to pray with the person concerned. If you are having trouble with someone in your church or group, try to pray with him about various needs and joys. This effort to share and understand will be rewarded by fellowship and a growing love.

The love of God believes the best about people, and discounts adverse reports and rumors. Love sympathizes and assists. Perhaps there are intense problems handicapping the person. Poor health may be dragging him down. Background environment or heredity may still control the individual. Prayer together can open the channel of love and wisdom from God to both.

Belief in the sovereignty of God enables us to rest in the confidence that He is in charge of all that is going on in the earth. Sometimes the devil seems menacingly near, but he is weak in comparison with the God who is in charge of our lives. Though Satan makes headway, he cannot overcome the Christian who is trusting God. He can say, "The Lord is in this," and look for the Lord's way out. Philippians 1:6 assures us that God has begun His work in us, and He will complete it.

Another step that develops love is personal interest in the welfare of others. This is shown by both words and deeds. Sincere attention builds a bond that involves us in other's lives. If someone's personality rubs against yours, ask questions about your common concerns and look for things to compliment. You'll find love sprouting from the interest, and you may receive love in return.

Some of us find it easy to make fun of people: the shape of their ears, the style of clothes, or the odd mannerisms. Jokes about others are good fun unless they wound the victim. Amy Carmichael said:

> "If I enjoy a joke at the expense of another, if I can in any way slight another in conversation or even in thought, then I know nothing of Calvary love. If I belittle those whom I am called to serve, talk of their weak points in contrast to what I think are my strong points; if I adopt a superior attitude, forgetting 'Who made thee to differ? What hast thou that thou didst not receive?' then I know nothing of Calvary love.

Another stimulus to love is to give something to another. There is a story of a husband and wife whose marriage was on the rocks. The husband never remembered anniversaries or birthdays, and he was always complaining. She became more and more discouraged. One day he inexplicably decided to bring her some flowers. It was so unusual that when he came to the door and held out the flowers she wept hysterically. "What a miserable day!" she moaned. "I've been having trouble with the children all day, the clothes washer broke, I burned the supper, and now you've come home drunk!" Don't wait so long to rebuild a relationship that your gift can't be believed! Give something of practical help or a memento that shows you care.

How blind we sometimes are to the plain words of Scripture! Jesus commanded the help of His people to one another by saying: "Inasmuch as ye have done it unto one of the least of these my brethren, ye have done it unto me" (Matthew 25:40). This is a revolutionary passage of Scripture, and if we let it penetrate our minds daily, it would change our lives. Our attitude toward the weak and the needy, God says, reveals our attitude to his Son. This should lead us to repentance. "He who loves not his brother whom he has seen, how can he love God whom he has not seen?" (1 John 4:20).

And have we forgotten what is called the Golden Rule? "Therefore all things whatsoever ye would that men should do unto you, do ye even so unto them: for this is the law and the prophets" (Matthew 7:12). This verse offers us a simple check on our speaking or acting: Would I enjoy this if it were directed at me? This would eliminate cruel gossip and future judgment.

The Bible tells us we are to correct someone in the spirit of love when it is necessary. "Brethren, if a man be overtaken in a fault, ye which are spiritual" — which excludes quite a few Christians — "restore such an one in the spirit of meekness; considering thyself, lest thou also be tempted" (Galatians 6:1). Amy Carmichael wrote: "If we can go to someone to correct them without a pang in our hearts, then we know nothing of Calvary love." The love depicted in 1 Corinthians 13 allows no rejoicing hearts over the failure of another person. Love never speaks with the attitude: "I told you so; you should have listened to me!" It sorrows with those who mourn, and lifts up those who fall.

In His love, God can transform sorrows and failure so we can help and comfort others. God, says Paul, "comforteth us in all our tribulation, that we may be able to comfort them which are in any trouble, with the comfort wherewith we ourselves are comforted by God" (2 Corinthians 1:4). How can a woman who has had four children, with no complications at birth and no problems as they have grown up, help a woman who has had three still births and now has a handicapped child? She has not been prepared for this opportunity. But a woman who has lost a child herself or has suffered deeply in some other way can communicate the love of God that she has experienced. She may speak directly, but with compassion, to the sufferer.

To rebuke and exhort another Christian is one of the hardest things to do properly. It is easier to overlook the fault, but love must correct at times. Amy Carmichael comments: "If I'm afraid to speak the truth lest I lose affection or lest the one concerned should say, 'You do not understand,' or because I fear to lose my reputation for kindness; if I put my own name before the other's highest good, then I know nothing of Calvary love."

Love acts. When I see a little child running toward a busy street, I do not just stand there and suggest: "Wouldn't it be better to stay on the sidewalk?" I move into action. I grab the child back from the street in order that its life may be saved. The Bible says that we are to snatch men from the fire of hell. To think such action too drastic is a misconception of love.

The love of Jesus was not of the Hollywood variety. His love led Him to serve. I believe it was also love that sent Jesus into the Temple to clean up the mercenary mess there and to chase out the greedy merchants with violence. It was love for righteousness; it was love for those who were being cheated. His love led to action all through his life.

Love grows — when it is exercised. Supplying all-conquering love is God's part; expressing love is our part. As we walk with God, He will make us confident "of this very thing, that He which hath begun a good work in you will perform it until the day of Jesus Christ" (Philippians 1:6). And God will work in the lives of others by love, for His perfect love never fails.

7

When I Am Weak...

Many young people begin Christian service believing that they are dedicated and keen Christians. They have been encouraged to think so by their complimentary friends or church officers. And perhaps they did rise above the average Christian in their surroundings. But service on the firing line makes them more and more conscious of Jesus' words: "Without me you can do nothing" (John 15:5).

All Christian workers come eventually — if they are honest — to the place where they can no longer casually affirm their dedication to the Lord. They realize only too well that they are not Hudson Taylor or George Müeller or C.T. Studd. The result may be extreme depression, since great exploits constantly elude them. They may conclude that there is no hope for them.

There is an antidote for this. Robert Murray M'Cheyne once said that for every look he took at himself, he took ten looks at the Lord Jesus. He had abandoned hope in himself, but his hope in Christ was boundless! For M'Cheyne and for us, total failure may be necessary to bring us to the realization our only hope is in Jesus! And it is not Jesus plus money, or

Jesus plus an efficient organization, or the proper equipment, but only Jesus!

Thanks to the Apostle Paul, we have an example who has proved this way to victory. "And he said to me, my grace is sufficient for thee; for my strength is made perfect in weakness. Most gladly therefore will I rather glory in my infirmities, that the power of Christ may rest upon me" (2 Corinthians 12:9).

When you are in a tight situation, when the demons of discord, criticism, misunderstanding, and confusion maul you in a pressure cooker, remember those words: *"My grace is sufficient for thee."* Without this knowledge and confidence, you cannot survive the warfare that awaits the disciple of Christ.

Can the cost of Christian warfare be less than that of nations in conflict? If it is, it is not warfare. Alexander Duff, the Scottish saint of God, knew the cost. Weeping as he faced a crowd, he asked if Scotland had any more sons to give. "When Queen Victoria calls for volunteers for India, hundreds respond," he reminded them. "But when King Jesus calls, no one goes." The silence was deafening. "If there is no one who will go," he continued, "then I will return. I will return and lay my bones by the Ganges, that India may know that Scotland has at least one who cares."

Whether we remain at home or go abroad, Christ's claim upon our lives is a call to battle. The enemy is powerful; he is dragging and tricking souls into hell; he is devastating the hopes and plans of men on earth. Yet Jesus can defeat him through any Christian who puts on the spiritual armor (Ephesians 6:11-18). Our hope, then, is in the all-sufficient Lord Jesus, not in ourselves. Whatever the circumstances: "My grace is sufficient for thee," promised God.

Someone has said that "grace is God's riches at Christ's expense." This definition underlines the great gift imparted to us by Christ. It is the riches of the infinite God, inherited through the death and resurrection of His Son. *It is all too easy to become indifferent to what Jesus did on the cross.* It is all too possible to gather thoughtlessly around the Lord's Table. When this happens, we void the riches of the grace of God!

There is another way of voiding God's grace: we do this by underrating it. If we get to the point of desperation and say, "O God, what's the use? I can't go any further — and you can't help me, either," we deny the grace of God. And just at that moment, we could discover His grace, His sufficiency, His life, and His power are available to take us through. This is tragic and sinful.

The demands and standards of Christ are admittedly extreme — in fact, impossible. But Jesus does not ask us to live the Christian life; He asks us to let Him live it in us. There was no grace for the self-righteous man who prayed "Thank you, Lord that I'm not like the rest." But there was grace for the man who wept, "I'm a sinner; Lord, have mercy on me!" The complete sufficiency of the Lord Jesus Christ makes up for our deficiency. We cannot earn His grace; we can get it only by coming empty to the cross.

Paul speaks an amazing truth in Colossians 2:9-10: "For in Him (Christ) dwelleth all the fullness of the Godhead bodily. And you are complete in Him." Complete! Do we realize this when we strive to build a reputation? Do we realize it when someone deprives us of recognition? Do we realize it when we feel uncomfortable in a group? Perhaps we feel worse when we suffer persecution or ill health for serving God. Or we may languish in jail for righteousness' sake. Our plans fail; our witness is rejected. How do we feel then?

You are complete in Christ! Our completeness is not in Christ plus friends, Christ plus service, Christ plus position, Christ plus converts. We are complete only in Jesus! In Him is all the fullness, so Jesus is all that we need. Everything else may fail us; Jesus will never leave nor forsake us.

Whatever arises that might discourage us, we can echo with the conviction of Paul: Jesus is sufficient for that, too. The question is not in His sufficiency, but only in our trusting Him. We cannot go on, we just will not make it! We may want to quit: the Lord is asking too much of us! Each time, *He is sufficient.* He says to us, "You are complete in me." We have been made acceptable to God in Christ the Beloved One.

We all seek acceptance; all of us want to be needed, liked, cared for. If we expect we are going to meet the ideal husband or wife to meet those needs, we are going to be disappointed. Not even a husband or wife can fulfill our heart's deepest longings, because we were made for God. Only He can reach down and fill that deep void; only He can satisfy.

In Jesus Christ, we have been accepted by God now. We have been accepted, not by some social group, but by the infinite God. We have been accepted, not in our spotted virtue, but in the perfect Lord Jesus Christ. With this confidence motivating us, nothing in the heights or depths, in life or death, nor in the whole universe can stop us, for nothing can withstand Him. His grace, abundant and overflowing, is ours — if we will receive it.

8

Steps to Revolution!

Having read these pages, you might be asking yourself: "What do I do next?" To read about the all-sufficiency of Jesus Christ is one thing; to obtain and experience it in your own life is another.

More than anything, this book is a plea and a guide for reality in the Christian life. The standard of vital Christianity described in these pages will not be reached easily. It will not occur through a short prayer of commitment or by any kind of crisis experience. God may use a crisis to jolt a Christian into action, but *a crisis plus a process* is necessary to keep him moving as a revolutionary disciple of Jesus Christ.

If this book is to be significant to you, you must *"declare a personal revolution."* This will take all your dedication and the application of every means of grace offered in the Word of God. There cannot be a revolution for those who merely "play the game" or go through the motions. Nor is revolution possible for the Christian who is not willing to deny self, take up his cross daily, and follow Jesus.

We are not ready for revolution if we have not yet seen the spiritual schizophrenia within and around us.

God must convince us that "the heart is deceitful above all things, and desperately wicked." Spiritual fog seeps into our hearts from the world, and only God can dispel it in response to earnest prayer.

To be ready for revolution, we must accept the blame for not living a dynamic Christian life. Christ lives within the Christian and *He* is the revolutionary. We must be willing to die to self-interests and self-determination and let Christ live His life through us.

Many Christians are entering the ministry and the mission fields and other places of Christian service without being spiritually prepared. We must realize that we are in dangerous territory if our service for God is taking us beyond our experience of God. Satan waits there to attack us — and we are very vulnerable. The revolutionary spiritual life issues from a deep relationship and experience with God, who makes the disciple a faithful soldier of Christ.

I am absolutely convinced that Christians who take the following steps to revolution will find that they "work". They work because Christianity works. These steps are basic biblical principles which Jesus Christ and the apostles repeatedly emphasized to those who wanted to be disciples of Jesus.

1. A revolution in our prayer life. One of the most depressing signs in the Church today is the lack of prayer, both in private and in groups. It is almost incredible to see how little the average evangelical church relies on prayer for doing God's work. When there is a prayer meeting, a small minority of the people are involved. Nights of prayer, home prayer meetings, days of prayer and fasting — so much a part of the early Church — seem nothing more than Christian relics today. Because people are busy, they think they are too busy to pray. The Church has sought innumerable substitutes for prayer to accomplish work that can be done *only* through prayer.

If we are serious about being spiritual revolutionaries, we must determine to learn how to pray! There are many excellent books on the subject, but there is no substitute for getting on our knees and starting to pray. Samuel Chadwick said, "The one concern of the devil is to keep the saints from prayer. He fears nothing from prayerless studies, prayerless work, prayerless religion. He laughs at our toil, mocks at our wisdom, but trembles when we pray."

The mountain peak of our prayer life will be worship. Specific times should be given each day to climbing the summit of spiritual reality through worship, praise and thanksgiving. King David declared, "I will praise the name of God with a song, and will magnify him with thanksgiving. This also shall please the Lord better than an ox or bullock that hath horns and hoofs" (Psalm 69:30, 31).

Reality in worship will create a spiritual revolution in the inner man, the likes of which few people seem to have experienced in the twentieth century. It will not be attained in a year or two, nor perhaps in ten or twenty years. However, since this is the highest calling of the Christian, it is worth any number of years to learn reality in daily worship. There is no more important aspect of spiritual revolution than this.

There is a sense in which we can "pray without ceasing" and offer prayer and praise to God at any time of the day. Yet there is also a need for separating ourselves from other humans and being alone with God. The entire Church and the cause of Christ around the world is suffering for lack of this kind of prayer. If the only response made to this book were a determination to take a definite time each day for prayer, and feasting on God's Word, the book would be eminently successful. For through prayer, we can come to see the other principles of spiritual revolution which will lead us from victory to victory as God's Word is mixed with our faith.

2. A revolution in our Bible study. At any cost, spiritual revolutionaries must become "men of the Book." D.L. Moody declared, "Either sin will keep you from this Book, or this Book will keep you from sin." Most Christians place a low value on memorizing and meditating on the Word of God. In contrast, Muslims by the thousands leave their universities with the whole Koran memorized. Actors and actresses memorize thousands of lines to earn fame and wealth. Despite the spiritual rewards promised for students of God's Word, few Christians seek them. The result is churches peopled by spiritual dwarfs, some having been "growing" ten or twenty years in the faith.

In some cases spiritual dwarfs become leaders of the congregation, and the contrast with New Testament churches is shocking. If anyone points this out, he is regarded as a fanatic, an extremist, or a meddler.

On the other hand, I have found increasing numbers of believers around the world who are tired of eating spiritual breadcrumbs and want to get into God's Word in a new and revolutionary way. The important thing, however, is not so much our "getting into the Word of God" as "the Word of God getting into us"! This means we must engage in more than Bible reading; we must meditate intensively on the Word of God, as the Psalmist instructs in Psalm 119:9,11.

Our Bible study must be as honest and unprejudiced as possible. We cannot come to the Word of God with our favorite viewpoint and expect the Bible to shed new light. We must come to the Scriptures in humility and openness, and attempt to obey in our daily living each truth we find there.

An evangelist has warned: "We have taken the Word of God, the Sword of the Spirit, and used it to carve one another up instead of going forth in a great offensive in the name of Christ." How much easier it is to go to war over pet doctrines and favorite verses rather than continuing to receive the whole counsel of God, and advancing against the enemy.

We must not only determine to obey those verses we enjoy, or that strike us as being important, but we must be ready to obey verses that sometimes strike us in the opposite way.

We are sometimes eager to accept those verses that speak about blessing and to neglect verses that speak about suffering. We welcome the first part of 1 John 3:16, "Hereby perceive we the love of God, because He laid down His life for us" —and the rest trails through and out of our consciousness: "... and we ought to lay down our lives for the brethren." The next admonition also gets scant attention: "But whoso hath this world's goods, and seeth his brother have need, and shutteth up his bowels of compassion from him, how dwelleth the love of God in him?"

This is also God's Word! What excuse do we have for our failure to "love not merely in word but in deed and in truth"? Obedience here is revolution!

3. A revolution of discipline. For many, discipline is an unpleasant word. Yet church history shows no undisciplined man or woman who amounted to much for Christ. The basic support of discipline is motivation, and the best motivation is the constraining love of Christ.

Christ said, "If ye love me, keep my commandments." He also said, "If ye continue in my words, then ye are my disciples indeed." This is critical, as we can realize from Paul's concern in 1 Corinthians 9:26,27:

> "I therefore so run, not as uncertainly; so fight I, not as one that beateth the air: but I keep under my body, and bring it into subjection: lest that by any means, when I have preached to others, I myself should be a castaway."

Paul was disciplined but he recognized the danger of slipping and falling into sin. True discipline is possible only because of the promises of God. We find ourselves unable to keep a particular commandment or engage in a form of self-discipline, but we can be sustained by such a promise as; " I can do all things through Christ which strengtheneth me" (Philippians 4:13). For every battle and difficulty in life, there is an assurance of God's grace and sufficiency we can claim.

We are hearing more and more in Christian circles about a victorious life being attained through a particular sanctification theory or crisis experience which launches an effortless joyride with God. But for every Bible verse that speaks of rest, abiding, trusting, and allowing God to work through you there is another word nearby that speaks of battle, testing, obedience, and the need to present our bodies as a living sacrifice to do God's will. These are complementary and essential for the balanced life.

We do not pit Joshua against Caleb because they used different terminology and concepts to challenge the people to enter the Promised Land. The spiritual revolutionary learns the balance between God's action and his own. He depends on God's strength and wisdom to work out the salvation life within him.

For example, if you lie in bed tomorrow morning and pray that the Lord will lift you out of bed, you are likely to have a very late breakfast! The recital of "not I, but Christ" will bring about few changes unless you *move*. But when you move, the recognition of "not I, but Christ" will produce eternal results by God's Spirit.

One of the important disciplines is repentance. When we sin or fail, we can recover and go on if we immediately find forgiveness at the cross. Many a Christian has languished in depression and defeat because he hasn't learned the discipline of repentance. Not even Jesus Christ "felt" like going to the cross, but He went because He loved us and was obedient to the will of God. We may not "feel" like going to the cross, but we will because of our love for Christ. There we receive total forgiveness and joyous renewal that will enable us to live in discipline.

4. A revolution of love. Jesus Christ said that people would know Christians were His disciples because of their *love* for one another. The greatest indictment of evangelical Christianity is that Christians have failed to have this kind of love. Yet when I have seen this love in a few Christians, it has impressed me as the expression of genuine Christianity.

It is amazing to see how the Lord Jesus Christ can change an unloving, lost soul. In country after country I have seen the power of this revolution of love. If more of us would enter in and fan the flames of this love, I believe we would see spiritual revolution around the world in our generation. This does not necessarily mean the conversion of masses of people, but rather individuals everywhere transformed by the revolutionary principles of the New Testament and living them before others.

Unless we "declare a revolution" in the areas of life already mentioned, however, we will not see a revolution of love. For it is only as we get to know God at a deep level and trust Christ to work through us that we can receive and demonstrate revolutionary love. Until we do experience this love, the spiritual revolution will not reach very far.

Nothing obstructs revolutionary Christianity like the opposite of love: resentment, envy, anger, fear, jealousy, and hatred. The mutual toleration evidenced in handshakes after the typical Sunday morning church service also falls far short of the revolutionary love that unites brethren in dynamic fellowship. Yet a greater display of interest in one another is not the real answer; revolutionary love is the outcome of obedience to and communion with Christ.

The greatest possible impact on the world would be made if Christians of many races, backgrounds, churches, and temperaments were working together in love and harmony with Jesus as King and Lord. The Bible says, "Love casteth out fear," and we could move forward on that promise, finding that divine love would cast fear out of our hearts — the fear of people we do not understand, who are from a different race, or who worship differently. We must break out of our cliques and work with all of God's people. We must unite under the banner of Christ's love and the cardinal doctrines and principles of New Testament Christianity. The pride that scorns Christians outside "our group" will have to die at the cross before we can join in revolution. If any of us has received more light, exercised more gifts, or been granted more recognition, it should be demonstrated by more humility and more love.

This is the essential principle of Christian living and spiritual revolution; without it, there is no power.

5. *A revolution of honesty.* Spiritual honesty is one of our greatest needs. We evangelicals have grown accustomed to our religious masks, pretending to be one thing while living quite another. It has continued so long that we hardly know now where reality is. Can you imagine what a revolution of honesty would do in our churches? If we were honest, many of us would have to change the words of "Onward Christian Soldiers" in somewhat the following manner:

Backward Christian soldiers, fleeing from the fight,
With the cross of Jesus nearly out of sight;
Christ our rightful Master stands against the foe,
But forward into battle we are loathe to go.

Like a mighty tortoise moves the Church of God;
Brothers, we are treading where we've often trod,
We are much divided, many bodies we,
Having different doctrines, not much charity.

Crowns and thrones may perish, kingdoms rise and wane,
But the Church of Jesus hidden does remain;
Gates of hell should never 'gainst that Church prevail,
We have Christ's own promise, but think that it will fail.

Sit here, then, ye people, join our useless throngs;
Blend with ours your voices in a feeble song.
Blessings, ease and comfort, ask from Christ the King,
With our modern thinking, we won't do a thing.

These words might seem harsh, but you will find stronger words in the New Testament:

> "I know thy works, that thou art neither cold nor hot: I would thou wert cold or hot. So, then, because thou art lukewarm, and neither cold nor hot, I will spew thee out of my mouth. Because thou sayest, I am rich, and increased with goods, and have need of nothing; and knowest not that thou art wretched and miserable, and poor, and blind, and naked" (Revelation 3:15-17).

We must declare war on the kind of self-deception described in these verses. To do this, we must determine to become spiritually honest. We must face ourselves as we are, and we must allow God to begin to bring revolutionary changes. Many of us are trying to live at a particular spiritual level when we know we are nowhere near it! This leads to all kinds of unreality, confusion, and sometimes even to nervous breakdown.

Sometimes the Christian most anxious to improve his spiritual life ends up with the greatest problems — because he tries to make the changes himself. The need is not for spiritual extremists, but for spiritual revolutionaries who know the reality of spiritual balance. The spiritual revolutionary knows that according to Ephesians 1:6 he is fully accepted in the Beloved, and therefore he ceases striving to gain merit through his spiritual activity. He recognizes that he is a sinner, but in Christ he is a victor.

Christian leaders may fall into this trap quicker than the average Christian. When Christians make heroes of leaders, they may feel forced to act out their roles while despising their hypocrisy. It is a very unhealthy and precarious route to follow.

One of the reasons many Christian young people forsake the church and their parents is widespread spiritual pretense. A normal young person understands failures are inevitable, but continual inconsistency and spiritual dishonesty deeply confuse him. Some are so repelled by the double life that they "drop out." They would rather befriend an "honest" agnostic than live in the shadow of spiritual schizophrenia. A spiritual revolution may be necessary to recall these rebels to fellowship in the Church. I challenge the rebels to follow Christ and help spring this revolution.

6. A revolution of witness. When the revolution takes place in the areas described, it will spontaneously bring a revolution of witness. Half the world still remains in spiritual darkness as far as a knowledge of Jesus Christ is concerned.

When we have gone forth, we have often taken the nonrevolutionary form of Christianity. A.W. Tozer wrote: "The popular notion that the first obligation of the Church is to spread the gospel to the uttermost parts of the earth is false. Her first obligation is to be spiritually worthy to spread it.... To spread an effete, degenerate brand of Christianity to pagan lands is not to fulfill the commandments of the Lord."

Tozer was a twentieth-century prophet who spoke for God from the pulpit and through his books. If we put into practice the principles he set forth (allowing for human error), we would see a spiritual revolution. This in turn would lead to witnessing in every form which would gather many people into the Church of the Lord Jesus Christ. Down through history, men who had different theological perspectives have lived out the same kind of dynamic, revolutionary Christianity, and we should be able to lay down our doctrinal pop-guns and work together in world evangelism and spiritual revolution.

The Jehovah's Witnesses, with all their false doctrines, boast of being ninety percent mobile. That is, ninety percent of their membership is involved in definite outreach and witness. What can we say of our evangelical churches' mobility? In some churches it seems that only the pastor and perhaps a few others know how to win others to Christ. But the New Testament clearly teaches that each believer in Christ is a witness. The fact that people have come to Christ just through reading a piece of Christian literature should show us that no Christian need arrive in heaven without helping someone else get there. There are many ways to witness and though some ways may be better than others, the teaching of Scripture is that we primarily witness through life and through word. Far more than a crusade, a special project, or outreach program, true witnessing is a spontaneous outflowing of the indwelling Christ.

Let's stop clutching our weaknesses, shyness, lack of training, fear, or any other excuse and start believing the God of the impossible who specializes in using weak vessels. There is not a single Christian who cannot become an effective, revolutionary witness for Jesus Christ if he really wants to.

In conclusion, I have two requests. The first is by far the more important. I request you to unite with me in repentance at the foot of the cross and believe God to bring into our lives and the lives of other Christians a spiritual revolution. Let us bow in daily repentance, recognizing our failures and believing God for great and dynamic changes in the days to come.

Second, I ask you to take a few minutes and write to me, care of the publisher, expressing what you feel after reading these pages. Perhaps this could be your first act of discipline after reading this book. I have a tremendous desire to pray for anyone who truly wants a spiritual revolution in his own heart and life. Those of us who want spiritual revolution in the twentieth century must unite and work together toward this goal. God is on our side — and if He is for us, who can be against us!

The Revolution of Love

GEORGE VERWER

LITERATURE

First published 1989
Reprinted 1990 (twice), 1993 (twice)

ISBN: 18845-4307-3

Production by OM Literature
P.O. Box 1047
Waynesboro, GA 30830-2047
U.S.A.

Printed in Colombia

BUENA SEMILLA
Apartado 29724
Bogotá, Colombia

Contents

Acknowledgements

The message of this book would not have been possible without the dedication of my dear wife Drena, who has stood with me now in the battle for twenty-nine years.

My thanks also go to my editor, Dr. Ruth March, for her tireless efforts to transform my spoken messages into print.

Introduction

This book is a collection of messages that were first given in spoken form. Two are being republished, and the rest have never been published before. *Revolution of Love* was originally part of the 'orientation material' that was given to young people joining Operation Mobilization for one month summer campaigns in Europe in the early 1960s, and reflects many of the early emphases of OM. The emphasis of 'Spiritual Balance' came later on in the ministry of OM, and these messages were then published together in book form in 1977 under the title *Revolution of Love and Balance*.

The name 'Operation Mobilization' came from the vision that God gave a small group of students from Europe and America back in the late 1950's. We felt that if Christianity was a spiritual revolution, a 'revolution of love', then the important thing was to obey what the Lord Jesus had told us to do in living for Him and going and teaching people in all nations of the world to be His disciples. We felt that many of the young people who in those days were sitting in the large churches of the USA, Britain and Europe could be mobilized to tell those who did not know about the good news of Jesus Christ and the need for repentance and a personal faith.

I felt strongly about the need for prayer and evangelism because without the faithfulness of one elderly woman in the States I would never have known about the joy of knowing God in a personal way. I was brought up in a home where such things were not

talked about. Then, one day, I received a Gospel of John through the mail. This Christian lady had seen me going to my high school and had already started to pray that I should become a Christian.

She had to pray for several years before anything happened at all. Then, in March, 1955, the evangelist Billy Graham came to Madison Square Garden. For the first time I heard and responded to a clear message on the salvation that God has made available to us through Jesus Christ, and I surrendered my life to Him.

Some people ask if that sort of decision of total commitment can really last. I would like to tell you that what happened to me that night so many years ago has been a reality in my heart and life for every single day since. I can assure you that it is not some late adolescent escape from guilt, but it is a true, living and real experience with God Himself made possible through what Jesus Christ has done on the Cross.

When we presented the challenge of those who had never heard to the young Christians of the western world in the 1960's, they responded by the hundreds. Today, many thousands of young people have spent time with OM, as it is usually known, in one of the short-term or longer-term options, and 'OM graduates' are found in almost every Bible college or missionary society in the world.

The message contained in *A Wide Open Heart* was first given to a group of OMers and other Christian workers in Peshawar, Pakistan, early in 1988. The refugee crisis in Pakistan means that Christians from many different backgrounds and organizations are working together in service and evangelism, so that a broad-minded attitude is particularly important. We in OM have always taken a strong stand against extremism, and this plea to be open-hearted in the work of God reflects that view.

Real People, Real Power and *New Generation — Unfinished Task* were messages from OM's leadership training conference at Birmingham in March, 1988. This conference is not primarily for OM leaders but for young people in positions of responsibility in churches, and Christian campus organizations. I feel that these two powerful messages on discipleship and power in the Christian life, and on the challenge of missions in the world today, are relevant not only to these young people but to many in the church today.

Finally, *Accepting Yourself and Others* is taken from a seminar given to our local OM teams in Bromley, in the spring of 1988. This seminar helped to answer the need of many people to learn to accept their own personalities as God accepts them, and therefore to learn to accept other people in the same way.

I share these messages with you in the hope that as you study them it will help you to be a true spiritual revolutionary for Jesus Christ.

George Verwer
Bromley, Kent
January 1989

1

The Revolution of Love

JESUS CHRIST WAS A REVOLUTIONARY — the greatest and most complete revolutionary this world has ever known. Not a political revolutionary, but a spiritual revolutionary.

And I believe that Christianity is a 'revolution of love', a revolution that the Holy Spirit wants to bring about in our hearts and lives as He radically changes the way that we think and act. I am convinced that there is nothing more important in all the world than this.

As we see the state of the church worldwide and the state of many believers today, it is easy to become discouraged. We look for discipleship; we look for those who are working together in unity, in prayer, in power... and we see quarrels and divisions, complacency and mediocrity.

Many people are asking, "Why is the church in such a state? Why is Christianity today making so little impact?"

Some people think that somehow we have missed some essential teaching or experience, and if we can only rediscover this secret through new meetings and

books, deliverance and restoration will once again be brought to the church.

Now it seems to me that it would not be very fair of God to keep secret the most basic ingredient of Christian effectiveness. And, in fact, I do not believe this ingredient is a secret at all.

Let us look at Galatians 5:22-26:

> But the fruit of the Spirit is love, joy, peace, patience, kindness, goodness, faithfulness, gentleness and self-control. Against such things there is no law. Those who belong to Christ Jesus have crucified the sinful nature with its passions and desires. Since we live in the Spirit, let us keep in step with the Spirit. Let us not become conceited, provoking and envying each other.

The fruit of the Holy Spirit is love. But what does the Bible mean here by love? In 1 John we find a clear and simply stated definition: God is love.

In other words, true love is from God... it does not exist apart from Him. We know that God is One. Therefore, we cannot think of God the Father without thinking of love; we cannot think of the Lord Jesus Christ without thinking of love; we cannot think of the Holy Spirit without thinking of love. There is no separation. God does not send love. He does not manufacture it. God *is* love.

Now that appears to be a very simple statement, but I am convinced that only an extremely small percentage of believers have really come to grips with this truth.

The Basic Message

This is, I believe, the basic ingredient that is largely lacking in Christianity today, and the lack of it is the source of most of our problems. It is the cancer that is eating away at the church, but it is no secret. In fact, it is so non-secretive that it is written on almost every page of the New Testament. And yet, because our

hearts are so hard and cold, and because we are so self-centered we do not really believe that the basic message of the New Testament is *love!*

I am absolutely convinced that most of us miss this most obvious and often-repeated message, even while we are laying great emphasis on what is an 'orthodox' interpretation of the Bible; what is 'biblical teaching'.

Well, I would like to ask, "What *is* biblical teaching?" We have long discussions on the Second Coming, on the meaning of the crucifixion, on the Church, the Holy Spirit, and so on. But what about love and humility and brokenness? These usually go into a separate category, but I want to tell you that if your teaching does not include love, humility and brokenness, then your teaching is not biblical.

There are thousands, even millions, of people who claim to be 'orthodox Christians' because they cling to a certain set of beliefs in accordance with the Bible. They are aware that they do not practice much humility, but they do not think that makes them any less orthodox. They are aware that they do not really love other Christians (especially those who are different from them), but that does not cause them to think their teaching is not biblical.

They may admit that they know nothing of serving others and considering others better than themselves, and yet they consider themselves Bible-believing, orthodox Christians.

They could not be more wrong! This is not Christianity but a travesty of Christianity — thinking we can be orthodox without having humility, thinking we can call ourselves Bible-believing Christians though our lives do not show love or the other fruits of the Spirit. In fact, I believe that this is the greatest error that has ever hit the church of Jesus Christ!

Teaching cannot be separated from practical living. I cannot see Jesus Christ as some sort of split personality, partly doctrinal and partly moral, trying to bring

two separate realms of truth into our minds. He is not on one occasion satisfying our intellectual curiosity by teaching us things *about* God, and in a separate exercise meeting our moral need by trying to make us more like the character of God. You cannot have a correct understanding about God without wanting to live in a way that pleases God.

"Oh," someone says, "there is a good, evangelical Christian ...he has a very good understanding of the Bible. He doesn't have much love for others and he's not very humble, but he certainly understands the Bible." I tell you, he does not understand the Bible if he does not love other Christians. What do we read in 1 John 4:8? "Whoever does not love does not know God."

There is no more biblical teaching than love, and apart from love there *is* no biblical teaching. Love is the foundation of all other biblical teaching, and you cannot build the building of biblical truth without that foundation.

The Wise Man

Let's turn to some verses that teach us a lot about this revolution of love and how it works out in everyday life. James, chapter 3, beginning at verse 13; "Who is wise and understanding among you?"

Well, who *is* wise and understanding among you? Is it the person who knows all the answers? Is it the person who has the solution to every problem... the one who always knows which way to go, how to tell people about Christ, how to hand out literature? Is this the person who has true wisdom? Possibly. But not necessarily.

The passage goes on, "Let him show it by his good life, by deeds done in the humility that comes from wisdom." In other words, God says to the man who has the correct theory and who knows what the Bible teaches, "All right, let's see it in your life. First, above

everything else, let's see it lived out. If a man is truly wise, then he is truly humble.

Reading on in James, we find that certain things mean that a person cannot have true wisdom; just 'spiritual cleverness'. "But if you harbor bitter envy and selfish ambition in your hearts, do not boast about it or deny the truth." If we show off our great knowledge and understanding of the Bible, and yet our lives are not filled with humility and love, but with bitterness and pride, we are actually lying against the truth with our lives. And how do you think non-believers feel when they see Christians saying one thing and living another?

James goes on to explain bluntly where this false 'wisdom' comes from: "Such 'wisdom' does not come down from heaven, but is earthly, unspiritual, of the devil." It must indeed please the devil with the damage it can cause.

An Illustration

Let me illustrate this kind of 'spiritual cleverness' with an incident that occurred in our work some time ago. A team member made a mistake when doing something practical. Naturally, one of his colleagues was keen to put him right.

Very quickly he said, "This is wrong. You should not have done it that way." The first team member said defensively, "Well, I was told to do it that way." The second, even more heatedly, said, "Well, I know it is not right. This is what you should have done." And soon they had a full-scale argument.

Later on, I was able to have a talk with the one who claimed to be right. I said to him, "Do you still feel you were right in that situation?"

"Absolutely," he said. "I was right and everybody else knows I was right!" And, indeed, he had managed to convince everyone else that he was right — not only on the practical point but in the way he had acted.

Then I said, "Tell me, when you spoke to him, were you controlled by the Holy Spirit or by your emotions?"

He stopped at that and thought for a minute. "Well, I don't suppose that I was really what you would call controlled by the Holy Spirit."

I said, "Well, then, you were controlled by your emotions." He was a bit hesitant but said, "All right, I admit that I was controlled by my emotions and not by the Holy Spirit, but I was still right."

So I said, "But surely the word of God says that those who are controlled by their sinful nature cannot please God!" (Romans 8:8)

He wasn't right! The way I think, the way I believe Christ thought, the way I believe the New Testament teaches, he was absolutely wrong in the way he had acted, because even though he was telling what he believed to be the truth, he was saying it without love, and the Bible teaches that you cannot tell the truth without love and still please God.

We ask, "Is it true? Is it theologically accurate? Is it orthodox?" And all the time God is looking at the state of our hearts, and our lack of love for our brothers and sisters. I believe that the curse of today is orthodoxy without love, orthodoxy without power, orthodoxy without the life of our Lord Jesus Christ!

When we as Christians try to communicate in areas that have been traditionally Roman Catholic or Muslim or Communist, we must always remember that no matter how right we are about an issue, the minute we act without love, we are being controlled by our own nature and not living in Christ, and that is sin. No matter how much 'truth' comes from our mouths about the need for repentance and faith in Christ, and about the inability of any other religion or philosophy to bring people to God, if it is spoken without love it will not please God.

That is what the Bible is saying in these verses. This 'wisdom' that does not come with kindness and gentleness and love is not wisdom. It is unspiritual, devilish. Some of the most horrible and unbelievable situations can arise in the church amongst those who have 'lip truth' but do not live the truth.

The next verse says, "For where you have envy and selfish ambition, there you find disorder and every evil practice." Where there is no true love, where there is no true wisdom, you cannot hope to have Christians working together in an orderly way. In the work of Operation Mobilization we have seen again and again that no matter how much people know about the Bible, if they are not living it out in their lives there will soon be disorder, confusion and pain.

Pure and Peace-loving

True wisdom, on the other hand, will never bring confusion: "But the wisdom that comes from heaven is first of all pure" (verse 17a). God's wisdom is primarily not orthodox, but pure. And whenever what we say, and do, is not pure, then it is not from heaven, but is a mere earthly 'spiritual cleverness'.

God's wisdom is also peace loving (verse 17b). Alan Redpath says that when you know you are not controlled by the Spirit, when you know you are a little upset, then just do not open your mouth! I like the way he puts it: "At that moment, literally force yourself back into the will of God." Force yourself back into the will of God, and then speak. But never open your mouth when you are not controlled by the Spirit, for no matter how hard you try you will never speak with true wisdom.

How many times have you hurt someone because you spoke too soon? Husbands and wives, how many times have you hurt your partner because you did not keep quiet a few minutes longer, until you were in control of your tongue? I have lost count of the number

of times I could have kicked myself just because I did not wait a little longer before I spoke.

James reminds us, "The wisdom that comes from heaven is first of all pure; then peace loving, [then] considerate." Considerate wisdom — gentle, the King James version says. I wish many young people would study this verse. It is easy to be a 'keen Christian' when you are young — and we are grateful for that. When you are young and energetic it seems that the world is just waiting to be conquered in the name of Jesus Christ. You cannot imagine why it has taken so long.

But when we reach the age of thirty or thirty-five, or after the first child has arrived, suddenly it becomes a bit harder to raise the enthusiasm for yet another outreach or yet another meeting. Suddenly we are a bit more understanding of others and a bit slower to condemn them for their apathy. Finally, we have to admit that so often we have been working in the energy of our own nature. Youthful energy! Youthful enthusiasm! But where was the gentleness that should have gone with the energy? Remember, the wisdom that comes from heaven is always considerate of others.

How Do You Respond?

God's wisdom is also 'submissive'. Now this is an emotive word. Does the Bible mean we should be some kind of doormat for others to step on? Certainly not. In fact, when you look a little more deeply into the meaning of this word, you find that it could have been translated 'easily persuaded'. So 'submissive' in this context means that we should not be stubborn when we are wrong; that we should be easily taught and corrected.

How do you respond when, for instance, you are helping to make tea after a church meeting and someone says: "Oh, you shouldn't have used that water — it wasn't really boiling. Pour it all out and start again.

And why have you used these teaspoons? We always use the ones in this box..." are you willing to be corrected?

Or what if you have been playing the guitar for your music group in the morning service and someone comes up to you and says, "That chorus you were playing at the beginning was much too slow... and I don't like the one we finished with, it's too noisy for the older people. And the way you were standing was all wrong, we couldn't see your face at the back...." What would you say? You need to be close to the Lord to accept criticism, however well-meaning it may be.

I believe that one of the greatest tests in the Christian life comes when we are confronted with correction and criticism. When we are criticized, rightly or wrongly, then we must learn to lean, not on other people's opinion of our work, but only on Jesus. Possibly that is why God sometimes allows the props to be knocked from under us, and puts us under fire in the form of criticism. We need to learn to work only for His "Well done, good and faithful servant."

This passage gives us some other ways to test true wisdom. Next, James says, "the wisdom that comes from heaven is... full of mercy and good fruit, impartial and sincere." Full of mercy — towards those who are weak, those who are insecure, those who have done wrong; full of mercy and full of the fruit of the Spirit. It is impartial and sincere; without hypocrisy.

This is true biblical teaching — truly orthodox belief. And I pray that if anyone can show me that this is wrong thinking or that I am misinterpreting the New Testament, and that it is possible for me to understand the Bible without peace, purity, gentleness, and so on, that they will show me. But please do not try to tell me that some Christian you know has a good understanding of the Bible but a miserable, loveless life, because I will just not believe you. Biblical teaching and true, God-given wisdom always come with a Bible-linked life. And all true Christian work

will reflect this partnership of biblical teaching and biblical living.

Explosive Message

Perhaps the clearest explanation of what is meant by the 'revolution of love' is found in 1 John 3. This letter is so loaded with revolution and dynamite that, if taken seriously, it makes the writings of Karl Marx look like a damp squib.

I will never forget a young, red-hot Communist who came into our Operation Mobilization office in the north of England many years ago. We read this letter with him and showed him the teachings of Jesus, and two weeks later he got down on his knees in the kitchen and gave his life to Christ. I tell you, the message of 1 John could have been written yesterday, so relevant is it to today's generation!

Now let's see what God says to us through 1 John 3:11. "This is the message you heard from the beginning: We should love one another."

What are we as Christians trying to get over to people? Sometimes it seems that our first message is 'believe'. Believe in the Lord Jesus and you will be saved. Believe in the Lord Jesus and afterwards everything will be fine. But when I read the word 'believe' in the New Testament, I find something that is like an atomic bomb. When a man really believes in Jesus Christ, it is revolution becoming operative, a revolution of love. You cannot separate the one from the other.

We know that true belief must include repentance. But what does 'repent and believe' really mean? Does salvation come when we first believe, or only when we have shown God the evidence of our changed lives? The Bible teaches clearly that salvation comes through faith alone. But real belief brings revolution. It results in a changed life. There is no such thing as real belief which does not change the believer. "Believe on the Lord Jesus and you will be saved." Doing good

will never save you, no matter how hard (or long) you work, or how much you achieve. But when you have believed, you are going to do good as a result, because the Holy Spirit, who lives in you as a Christian, wants to do good through you.

The Holy Spirit

Many years ago, when the gifts of the Holy Spirit were not talked about in most churches as freely as they are now, a friend came to me with stories of wonderful experiences some people had had in the Holy Spirit. I had to admit that I was a bit skeptical. I asked her, "When the Holy Spirit works in such a mighty way, shouldn't the people who have had such experiences afterwards be filled with love and joy and peace? Shouldn't they leave everything they have for Christ's sake, as we are told the early Christians did in the book of Acts? Shouldn't they even be willing to lay down their lives for others?"

Now I think my friend knew perfectly well that not all the people who had had these experiences 'in the Spirit' showed the evidence of a 'revolution of love' in their lives, and that some Christians who did show this evidence had never had this sort of experience. So she said to me, "Sometimes the Holy Spirit comes just to give us joy and a wonderful experience of blessing." I said to her, You mean that sometimes the Holy Spirit comes apart from his holiness?" And she had no answer to that.

I strongly believe that all Christians should seek to be filled with the Holy Spirit. But I tell you, the Holy Spirit does not come apart from His holiness. The emphasis is not on 'Spirit' but on 'Holy', and He cannot divide up His gifts and His character. Therefore, it is possible to measure people's true depth of experience with the Spirit (although it would be more correct to say the Spirit's experience with people) by the way that they live day by day.

You cannot separate the word 'believe' in its biblical context from the word 'love'. Don't try! How many men are there in our churches, leaders some of them, who speak to a congregation from the Word of God, but in their homes know nothing more about loving their wives than the man in the next house who cannot stand his! And they go on and on continuing to think they are spiritual men with just a besetting sin of not being able to really love their wives. I find this absolutely heart breaking! To me it is completely incompatible to say that you are a spiritual person and then not be able to get on with your family or even your neighbor!

If your 'besetting sin' is that you cannot love people, you are in serious trouble. I do not mean to say that it will always be easy to love people, or that you will not have battles about it. In fact, you will find that the devil will fight you tooth and nail in this area, often twenty-four hours a day. But this should not discourage you, for the Word of God clearly teaches that we are to love one another.

We cannot have fellowship with God without having fellowship with our brothers and sisters in Christ. We cannot love God without first loving our fellow Christians. Look at 1 John 4:20:

> If anyone says, 'I love God,' yet hates his brother, he is a liar. For anyone who does not love his brother, whom he has seen, cannot love God, whom he has not seen.

The popular idea today seems to be that if we love God enough, we will eventually love our brothers and sisters in Christ. But this is not what the verse says. It states clearly that if there is any brother or any sister who we do not love, actively, operationally, then our relationship with God is seriously wrong.

I am convinced that many of our prayers do not get any higher than the ceiling because of our lack of love and hardness of heart. If some of the prayers we hear in prayer meetings today were being answered, the

world would have been evangelized long ago. Fantastic things are asked of God. "Lord, we claim this country for you." "We believe, Father, that you will open a way into China." "Lord, we trust you to bring a hundred new people to the meeting tonight." And on and on we go, and yet all the time there are other Christians in the same prayer meeting whom we cannot stand. Oh, not that we don't love them... we would just rather not sit next to them. Of course we don't hate them — it is just that our personalities conflict!

Love Your Enemies

There are dozens of watered-down phrases for not loving other people. "Oh, I love him in the Lord, but I don't like his mannerisms... Susie is all right, but she is so hard to get to know... So and so has emotional problems, and such and such comes from such a *difficult* background...."

In the sight of God it is all hypocrisy. God never said in the Bible, "Love your brother if he is a keen Christian, well-dressed, a good evangelist... and if he gets on with you." No! In fact, Christ told us in the Sermon on the Mount that real love does not begin until we love our enemies!

This whole concept of loving our enemies is, for the average person of today, nothing but an outdated theological phrase, so impossible for human nature to attain that it is often not taken seriously even among Christians.

We know so little of it, so little of really loving people who cannot tolerate us, who speak evil of us, spite us, do not like us or the way we operate. Christians who live in cultures that are opposed to all Christian work and often all foreigners must learn the hard way what loving their enemies really means, if they are to go on loving even those who persecute them for Christ's sake. Meanwhile we in the West often cannot love even the people around us, who do us no harm at all!

Some time ago, someone told me flatly that he loved everybody. I said to him, "I find that hard to believe." But he was insistent that he loved everybody. Now I happened to know of at least one person to whom he didn't bother to say "hello" in the morning. He could pass this person several times a day, never showing kindness — not a smile. So I mentioned this person's name and asked "Do you really love him?" He said, "Of course I do. Well, I mean, I love all the believers."

It was all in the head! There is no love without action. Potentially that Christian may have loved everybody. Theoretically he may have loved everybody. But it was not a reality.

God's Work

Who is it that brings about this revolution of love? When you became a Christian, the Holy Spirit of God came to live within you, with all His potential for this tremendous life of love. The Holy Spirit is there, just waiting to take possession of you and make you more loving. He is just waiting to move you to volunteer to do some shopping for the older people in your church, or to help clean out the gutters. But what happens? Our pride, stubbornness, and self-centeredness soon get in the way and stop the action of the Holy Spirit in our lives.

Jesus Christ said, "Love your neighbor as yourself." Now, it's very nice that we Christians have been given the truth. But what has been the result in the practical realm? What has it been in India, for instance? Certain missionaries went with their heads in the clouds, taught, "Love your neighbor as yourself", but then shut themselves away from the people in their missionary compounds, and put locks on all the doors.

And in Africa, what have been the results? Well, in many places, the missionaries have said, "We love our neighbors as ourselves. But, well, the colored people had better use the back doors, and clean the houses, and be the nannies for the little white children."

What, then, does all this talk about love really mean? "Love your neighbor as yourself". Well, how do you love yourself? How did you love yourself this morning? You got out of bed groggily, wiped all the sleep out of your eyes, went to the mirror and said, "Oh, how I love you! You are so wonderful; I love you, I love you, I love you so much! Did you? Well, if you do that too many mornings someone might call in a psychiatrist for you. That is not the way we love ourselves! That is the way we love our neighbors. "The Lord bless you, dear brother. Yes, yes, the Lord bless you. The Lord do wonderful things for you!"

We sign our letters "love in Christ" and think, "Well, that's another one out of the way." But that is not the way we love ourselves. Perhaps we can understand love better if we use the word 'care'. You have been caring for yourself all day long, ever since this morning when you woke up and your self-love automatically went into action. You had a wash, maybe used a few creams and lotions, and put on the proper amount of clothes to keep your body warm. Shortly after getting out of bed, you had a little pain in your stomach — very slight, but enough to get you into action. Immediately you started toward the kettle and the cereals and bread and jam.

If you are really honest you will probably have to say that as you came to the table you were not wondering if you could make some coffee or tea for anyone else, or if you could make a start on the washing-up. No. You sat down, and, noticing that there was no margarine on the table, you began to look for some in the fridge. You were taking care of yourself automatically.

I am not saying that this is wrong. Neither does Jesus. It is wonderful that Jesus knows all about us; all about the human mind. If we could only grasp this truth, we could burn most of the psychiatry books in a big garbage can.

God doesn't say that you should not love yourself. But He does say that you should love your neighbor in the same way as you love yourself. He does not say that you should not have breakfast, but He does say you should be concerned about your neighbor's breakfast as well.

I pray that the Spirit of God will show you what this revolution of love really is — what it means to obey the command of Jesus Christ to love your neighbor from the time you get up in the morning until you go to bed at night. Only this will make an impact on such a materialistic age as this one! Our books and leaflets will not do it. Our Bibles will not do it. Jesus said, "All men will know that you are my disciples if you love one another." Not if you know all about the Bible and are fired with great enthusiasm. No! They will know it if you love one another. This is the greatest challenge in the word of God — to love people as Christ loved them, to love them as we love ourselves, to care for people as we care for ourselves.

Surrendering Everything

The only logical outcome of such love is to surrender everything to God. I believe that when someone falls in love with Jesus, it can be compared in some ways to a young man falling in love with a girl he has dreamed about all his life. The day they are married, he transfers his bank account and puts it in her name, and he takes out an insurance policy in her name. In other words, because he loves her, he gives her all he has.

A lot of Christians have trouble with this sort of teaching. Anything that involves money or possessions is very sensitive, and I do not want to judge or condemn anybody. Christians have very different ideas about what is meant by 'stewardship' of money and possessions and what is meant by 'giving up everything'. One Christian will sell his home and give the money to missions or to the poor. Another will keep a beautiful home and use it to show others the gift of hospitality.

I am not saying that God cannot use your possessions for His work and for His glory, once they have been surrendered to Him. But I am saying that we must first give all control of our possessions and our money to God. I know that it is difficult. Often we hold back because we have not yet learned to trust God with our whole lives. It is easy to sing "Jesus, I love you," and hard to hand over a bank account. I believe that often those who hold back have not yet fallen in love with Jesus Christ. Once our relationship with Him is right, we are no longer afraid of His control. Then we can lay everything at His feet.

The man who does not know the joy of giving has not yet begun to live, for it is, just as the Bible says, more blessed to give than to receive. It is a revolutionary principle of life that our greatest joys come from giving. It is completely contrary to our human nature. By nature we grasp everything to ourselves and we become the center. But when we become Christ centered, it is just like a centrifugal force, like a whirlwind throwing everything outward and leaving Christ alone, our one supreme love.

"Love your neighbor as yourself," said Jesus. And on another occasion he illustrated in the parable of the Good Samaritan who he meant by our neighbor and what he meant by love. Care for your neighbor as you care for yourself. That is why I find it hard to eat breakfast without praying for India, why I find it hard to take a piece of bread and a sip of tea without a pain in my heart for those who have no food.

We who claim to have the truth, we evangelicals, we Bible believers, have become hardened to the need of mankind. In recent years 'Live Aid' and 'The Race Against Time', which are not even specifically Christian, have overtaken many Christian groups in mobilizing aid for the starving in Africa and Asia. Sometimes I feel ashamed of the complacency of Christians, while these young people are making such efforts. If I asked you to distribute leaflets and promised to give you five cents a

leaflet, how many leaflets would you give out? If I said I would give you fifty dollars cash for every person you bring to Jesus Christ, maybe you would be motivated to go out and tell others about the gospel a little more! Is this really the way we should react? We all know it is not. No one can put a value on a soul.

We need to see where we are before God. Look at 1 John 3:14;

> We know that we have passed from death to life, because we love our brothers. Anyone who does not love remains in death.

That is quite blunt, isn't it? You say, "Oh, but I have been born again." But how were you born again? Putting your hand up in a gospel meeting did not make you born again. Saying "Jesus, I believe in you" did not make you born again. You were only born again and freed from spiritual death when you repented of your former lack of love and trusted in Jesus to give you His Holy Spirit, to produce His fruit of love in your heart for your brothers and sisters.

There are many people in our churches today who have made so-called decisions at some time in their lives, who have claimed to be Christians for many years and yet have never showed any evidence of repentance and whose lives are filled with a bitterness and a lack of love towards other Christians. This is a delusion — the largest, most detestable sugar-coated pill the devil ever gave out! There is no conversion without revolution. There is no conversion that does not produce the seed of a loving life, tiny though it be in the beginning.

Look at verse 16:

> This is how we know what love is: Jesus Christ laid down His life for us. And we ought to lay down our lives for our brothers.

This is how we know God loves us. This is how we know the love of God, the way we perceive it, the way we understand it. He laid down his life for us. He died for us; He did something. He did not sit up in glory and

sing, “My earthlings, I love you, I know you are mine.” He did not do that. That is what we do. We sit in our meetings and sing, “My Jesus, I love you,” and yet often we are not on speaking terms with the man in the seat beside us. Anyone who can sing that without going out from that meeting to show love in his life has passed through a religious pantomime that is an insult to Almighty God. And I am convinced that the world will never be evangelized unless we experience the love of God in our hearts towards others!

Now I am not going to give you some sort of list of steps to take so that you can experience the love of God. There are no short cuts in the Christian life. I am not going to tell you about some new gift or prayer style or experience that will lead you closer to God. These things have their place. But the first step to being filled with God’s love is to want it! Want to be like Jesus! Want to know this life-changing love! Want Him with a spiritual hunger that will get you so absolutely starved for God that eventually through knowing Him, His love will be poured out into your life!

> Blessed are those who hunger and thirst for righteousness, for they will be filled.
>
> (Matthew 5:6)

It is a universal law that when you want something badly, whether it is good or bad, if you continue to crave that thing, desire for it will take hold of your subconscious mind and eventually you will be motivated to get it. How many times has it happened that someone has asked you the name of a person and you have said, “I have his name right on the tip of my tongue… now what is it?” You were motivated to want to know that name. You tried again, “What is that person’s name?” And again, “Now what is his name?” And then you forgot about it for a while. You thought you had forgotten about it. But you had fed a wish into your inner being, into your subconscious mind, and the wheels started going. Ten minutes later, completely without conscious effort, what came into your mind? The person’s name!

This hunger this deep craving, can be used for evil as well as for good. Many years ago a young university student in Texas called Charles Whitman went up into a tower on the university campus one day and began to shoot people at random. This thought had come into his mind many times before. He had even mentioned it to his psychiatrist. But I am sure that the first time it occurred to him he was shocked and thought, "I could never do anything like that." Nevertheless, the thought continued to come to him more and more frequently. He suppressed it and suppressed it until finally it took possession of him totally and he was powerless against his craving.

This is what happens when you crave something. Every time you want something that is not of God, you sow a thought. Maybe you have a desire you wouldn't admit to your best friend or your husband or wife. Maybe it is new clothes, maybe it is marriage, maybe it is recognition. Perhaps it is even something legitimate, if God were to give it to you. But the craving is so strong in you that you begin to think, "Other people have it" and the seed of envy is sown in your heart. And then you think, "Why can't I have it?" and the seed of bitterness is sown.

Probably all of us have had thoughts like that at one time or another. But remember that if you go on allowing these thoughts to have possession of your heart and mind, they will take control of you. Soon the things of God will start to mean less and less to you, and in the end God may let you have your desire. But at what price?

Brokenness

In the same way I am convinced that if you want a life of love, if you want to be conformed to the image of Jesus Christ, if you want to join that remnant of people who are fed up with words, hymns and hypocrisy, if you want reality and revolution in your life, then you will get it. "Blessed are those who hunger and thirst for righteousness, for they will be filled."

It will take time. Perhaps you have heard this before and you say, "Last year I heard a message like this and I prayed and wept and rededicated myself before God. I said, 'Lord, I want to be loving, I want to be humble, I want to be gentle, I want to be a servant.'" And now you look back at the past year, and it is not very impressive. Do not be discouraged. What God wants of us is *brokenness.* He wants us to realize that in our own nature we cannot please Him, that we cannot love our brothers and sisters, that from the time we get up in the morning until we go to bed at night we live a life of utter selfishness, except when God interrupts us. Do you want this? Do you want to know something of loving your enemies? Do you want to know something of being a servant, something of being easily taught and corrected, of weeping for people who are without food and without Christ?

I will never forget a one day campaign we had in Bombay, when we were challenged to distribute half a million Christian leaflets in one day. After we had distributed some four hundred thousand leaflets throughout the day, we then had a meeting in the evening. And as we closed that meeting we said that if anyone was motivated to go back into the streets with leaflets, we still had a few left — about a hundred thousand! There were several volunteers. I had absolutely no desire to go out that night with more leaflets. It was 11 p.m., we had started the day at 5 a.m. and I had worked through the night before on the maps of the city. I was tired. I did not feel any love tingling through me. And as I started out, I just had to stop where I was and turn my eyes towards Jesus. I saw Him walking an extra mile for me — I saw Him going up Calvary's hill to the cross for me. That was love! It was action. And I said to myself that if Jesus could go the extra mile for me, then surely He would help me go the extra mile for those others whom He loved. Love is action! "If you love me, keep my commandments."

We went out into the streets of Bombay again, and around midnight I could see for about a quarter of a

mile in front of us thousands of men and women sleeping on the pavement. I've never before seen such a sight in my life. I had two big bags filled with leaflets, and for the first time in my life, I went from bed to bed, giving out leaflets!

This world in which we live is a sick world. It is a world of misery and tragedy such as most of us cannot begin to imagine. Millions are sleeping on pavements, starving to death, knowing nothing of the love of God for them. The church sings, "My Jesus, I love you". And at the same time a couple of thousand of people a day slip away into eternity. And we say that we love them. I say we don't. If we loved them with Christ's love, we wouldn't stop until we had sold a million books and distributed a hundred million leaflets and laid down our lives in every kind of service and action to help them. And as we did it, our tears would bathe these lost souls. I know too little about it. I have wept little over souls and much over my unloving heart. But I can say right now before God, *"I want it!* You can take all that I have! You can take my family (and I do not say this lightly), *but I want a life of love! I want God!"*

If you can say this with me, I believe that God will answer you! But if what you want is not God but Christian service, Christian activity, or Christian fellowship, no matter how good those things may be, then I do not believe you will ever be truly satisfied.

Lord, we cry to You to teach us to love, to break us of self, pride, stubbornness, that the love of Christ, poured out into our hearts through the Holy Spirit, might be operative daily, hourly, moment by moment.

We cry to You to teach us to love our enemies, to love our critics, not in word, but in deed also. We cry to You that we want this life of love, and we want You, for You are love!

Amen.

2

Spiritual Balance

LEARNING ABOUT THE REVOLUTION of love is something that is essential for all Christians, whether they have been following the Lord for five days or fifty years. Learning about the principles of spiritual balance is part of growing up as a Christian — moving towards spiritual maturity. In spiritual balance, biblical passages that give different aspects of the truth are kept together; not being watered down, but seen in context and in the perspective of God's whole revelation.

Spiritual balance, like spiritual revolution, is something that must be real for each one of us. If we only understand the principles of it in our heads, then our discipleship will not withstand the test of time and suffering. I am completely convinced that discipleship is not just for 'full time' Christian workers. Discipleship is for every believer. Discipleship is not just for people who are living in a Christian community or a Bible college. It is for believers everywhere. Discipleship is not a set of rigid rules. The principles of discipleship are more flexible and adaptable than many of us would dare to admit.

The unreal expectations of a few Bible verses taken out of context can lead people into spiritual frustration. Only by balancing one strong biblical truth with another will we come to spiritual reality.

Flexibility

The first area of conflict which often arises with keen, young Christians is that of flexibility; how much to try to convince others of the great teaching they may have received or the great experiences they have had, and how much simply to accept all Christians as they are. This is a conflict that may appear when young Christians have been for their first period of training with Operation Mobilization; or their first term with a college Christian Union; or their first Bible conference. Naturally, they may come back brimming with ideas to their home churches and begin to tell much older Christians just where they have been going wrong and how they should change. And just as naturally, the older Christians may react with some resentment.

This is a situation in which the need for balance is obvious. It is good for young Christians to have strong beliefs, and to be constantly learning and sharing what they have learned. But what happens when others are not so keen to listen?

As disciples of Christ, our chief rule must always be love, and love brings with it sensitivity to the needs of others. When we are in a church meeting or committee, and we find ourselves disagreeing violently about some matter of priorities or finance or church politics, and we feel the anger welling up within us, love restrains us. Love causes us to think before we speak. Most of us realize our tongues run faster than our brains, and that this can get us into trouble. True disciples are adaptable and flexible, although they do not compromise their beliefs.

If you spend time working with any Christian group you may find that you build up strong convictions on

minor issues, just because that is the way that group does things. But if you then go on to join another group, or return to work in your local church, you may find they have different convictions on these points, or that they do not consider these things important. This can become very frustrating, and may place a barrier between you and your new area of work and Christian service, unless your attitude is one of spiritual balance. Unless you are flexible, adaptable and loving, you will not be able to fit into another fellowship easily.

There is nothing wrong with having strong convictions, so long as we remember that we are still learners. A humble attitude will stop us thinking that we have the answers to every situation, and make us flexible to the convictions of others.

God uses men of completely opposite convictions. There is one man of God who visited us on the MV *Logos* once to do some preaching, and during his sermon smoked a pipe all the time. Now this is something that most of us involved in OM would find completely unacceptable. Yet, although he believes and acts differently to us, he is a man who is being wonderfully used of God.

God is so great and so mighty that He will always carry on the work of His kingdom, and He will use people despite their mistakes, weaknesses, and even wrong ideas and minor beliefs. Sometimes we will have to say; "Others may, I will not." This is very different to saying, "I will not, so no one else will either!", which is using our own weaknesses to judge and condemn others.

Work and Rest

Another area in which Christians often have great difficulty is the need to strike a balance between working as hard as possible, and yet leaving time to be relaxed and rested. The importance of relaxation is becoming more recognized today. There have been too

many Christians, especially leaders, whose ministry or families have collapsed under the strain, simply because they never learned to relax.

Some Christians think that there is too much to do to relax; that if they are truly disciplined they should be able to work all the time. But this is not the way God has made us. A time of relaxation helps us to build up our physical, emotional and spiritual strength and power so that we can then go on to accomplish more in a week than we would otherwise have done in a month.

Different people relax in different ways. Some people need complete separation from work to relax. Some need a week's holiday every so often, others can just take off a few hours, while others can just change from one sort of work to another. Some people's attitude to work is much more relaxed from the start, and they never become so uptight as some others. We need to realize that it is God who is in charge, and that we are not indispensable.

When we can trust God enough to relax, we will become more, not less, disciplined. It is easy to produce a false discipline, working ceaselessly, and being present at every meeting, just to impress others. This sort of attitude should never be encouraged. God, who looks at the heart, knows whether our work is first of all for Him or for other people.

It is self-discipline that will last, not some discipline that is imposed by others. Of course there are times when we need to accept the discipline of the church or community. This is only part of our own self discipline. And of course there will be times when we fail and fall short of our own standards. But I know of no better way of learning than through failure.

Concern and Inner Peace

To be able to learn through failure takes another area of balance; the ability to balance concern and inner peace. It is good to be concerned that things are

done in the right way and that people are living in the right way, but it is not good to have unhealthy anxieties. If we know that we are working with God and that He is in control, it is possible to have peace within ourselves when other things are going wrong.

Without an inner compulsion to get things done in the best possible way, many Christian leaders would not achieve what they do for God. But that compulsion must not become an obsession; it must be kept under God's control.

If we do not learn to have inner peace when things go wrong, we will become impatient with those around us. Look instead at how the Lord Jesus dealt with His stumbling, fumbling disciples. They said and did many stupid things, but He did not become impatient with them, but forgave them everything.

Perfection Through Failure

When we learn to have inner peace because we know we are complete in God's own Son, we will be able to obtain a balance between aiming at perfection and coping with failure. To be perfect should be the aim of every true Christian; to live a life in the Spirit, not to offend anyone, to love everyone as Christ loves us, to do all things in the right way and to glorify God in our every action.

But each of us must also learn to accept failure, especially our own failures, mistakes and shortcomings. We must know what to do when we fail. Wallowing in 'repentance' that is mostly made up of self pity is not the answer, for it merely paralyzes our effectiveness. We refuse to get on with the work of God, imprisoning ourselves in a self-imposed purgatory, while the devil chuckles with delight.

Avoiding failure is not the answer either. Many Christians are so afraid of failure that they simply lower their aims. "We won't have a prayer meeting in case nobody comes." "We handed out leaflets last year and someone laughed at us, so we won't do it again."

To be afraid of failure in this way is to dishonor God. Fred Jarvis has said, "The greatest sin of Christians is not failure, but aiming too low." We must not try to diminish God by our own lack of faith. We must have high aims, but be able to accept our own failure.

Some Christians tend towards a perfectionist attitude, and may have impossibly high aims for themselves while worrying over every slip and fall. Others will simply avoid failure by compromising and lowering their aims so that they achieve nothing at all for God. The difference is often not one of spirituality, but of temperament. The only answer is to have spiritual balance.

Sometimes Christians live a whole day in frustration because they were unable to get their 'quiet time' first thing in the morning. They really believe that the devil is going to pounce on them extra hard. Actually the Bible does not even mention having a 'quiet time'. The devil is going to attack us anyway whether we miss our 'quiet time' or not. Let us aim for perfection, but not become obsessive over it.

We must learn to handle our mistakes. Sometimes our expectations are unreal. With young people who have not had much experience in Christian work, but who have read inspiring Christian books and been to impressive Bible conferences, there are bound to be disappointments and frustrations. These things are a normal part of the Christian life, particularly in a group situation.

We should learn to take Christian biographies with a pinch of salt. They are often so concerned to tell us all about this great man or woman of God that they select only the good points, leaving out the difficulties and weak points. This is particularly true of books written some years ago. The impression given is of a life free from any mistakes and failure, and this can be very discouraging to young people who then find that the Christian life is not quite like that.

The inner history of many missions and societies is not always pleasant and inspiring. Some of the greatest men and women of God had amazing inconsistencies and weaknesses. But God used them despite their mistakes, for in Christ, He made them perfect. In 1 Corinthians we read about unspiritual Christians in the New Testament. Yet Paul opens his letter by saying he is writing to those who are sanctified. It is clear from the letter that some of these people were living in sexual sin and doing all kinds of things against God, but the apostle Paul knew how to handle people's failures. He encouraged them to keep aiming for perfection, but he also showed them how to pick themselves up and keep going when they failed. This balance is the only way to achieve spiritual maturity.

Spiritual Maturity

There is a lot of spiritual immaturity in the Christian world in the realm of material possessions. It is amazing how easily we get the 'I want' bug, just because we see that someone else has something and not because we need it. Generally, if we really need something God will give it to us. But often it is only when we see somebody else with something that we suddenly realize we want it as well. We may start to envy someone else's food, or clothes, or music system. This is not genuine need; it is simply jealousy.

God's way is much more revolutionary than the materialistic way of life we are used to. The apostle Paul lived this out; he chose to go without some things that other Christians thought were essential. Don't base your spiritual life on even the most dedicated Christian you know. Base it instead on the word of God and what the Lord Jesus reveals to you. Perhaps the Lord has shown you things you should not do, such as drink alcohol or spend money on luxury items. Then you meet some apparently mature Christians who are doing these things. This can be most upsetting, and you may begin to wonder if you were right to obey God.

Firstly, remember that these Christians may not be as spiritually mature as they appear. Often people with strong, outgoing personalities gain reputations as keen Christians, when in reality they are depending on natural ability rather than a close knowledge of God. Secondly, remember that we all have strengths and weaknesses in different areas. Just because these Christians have a weakness in this particular area, does not mean that they are not strong in other areas. In fact, some Christians are able to stay close to God while doing some things that for most of us would cause problems. We must not judge others, but must obey what God shows us about the way to run our own lives.

Let us beware of getting worked up by the way people spend money. This is always a sensitive area. There are some people who will spend more money in one week for a hotel room and food than some of us would spend in a month. Yet God is using them. How can this happen? It can happen because God is sovereign, God is great, God is a God of love, God is a God of mercy, and He looks upon our hearts. Let us look to God and live our lives the way He shows us, being able to say, "Others may, I cannot." This is the sign of true spiritual maturity.

Spiritual Balance

Learning about spiritual balance enables us to learn to distinguish the difference between what is biblical principle and what is personal conviction. It is possible to find a Bible verse to support almost anything, but only if you are willing to take isolated Bible verses out of context.

Certain things we do in life do not come directly from biblical principles. The larger principle of love guides us to do things in the most convenient and practical way. If we are spiritually mature, we can accept this, even if it means things are not always done in the way that we would prefer.

Having a balanced attitude to important biblical principles leads us from spiritual immaturity to maturity; from frustration to fulfillment. Only when we learn to be adaptable yet strong in our beliefs; to work hard yet to relax in God; and to aim at perfection through failure, will we become effective and used by God.

Lord, teach us about spiritual balance. Let us not look to others for our example, but to You alone; learning to follow Your Word, not just the passages that we have selected to suit our own abilities or temperament, but in its glorious and complete whole.

Amen.

3

A Wide Open Heart

"*ALL MEN SHALL KNOW* that you are my disciples if you love one another" said Jesus (John 13:35). Is this the way the rest of the world looks at the Christian church? Or do they merely see divisions and intolerance, criticism and narrow-mindedness?

The narrow-mindedness of Christians is not a new problem:

> "Teacher," said John, "we saw a man driving out demons in your name and we told him to stop, because he was not one of us." "Do not stop him," Jesus said, "No one who does a miracle in my name can in the next moment say anything bad about me, for whoever is not against us is for us. I tell you the truth, anyone who gives you a cup of water in my name because you belong to Christ will certainly not lose his reward."
>
> (Mark 9:38-41)

Now the Bible teaches us that the way to God is a narrow road. And yet we do not have the right to try to make it narrower than it really is, by excluding everybody who does not think and believe exactly as we do. Sometimes we are so narrow-minded and so rigid that our hearts are not wide open to what God is

doing. Our hearts are closed, as Paul wrote to the Christians at Corinth:

> It is not we who have closed our hearts to you; it is you who have closed your hearts to us. I speak now as though you were my children: show us the same feelings that we have for you. Open your hearts wide! (2 Corinthians 6:12-13, GNB)

Narrow-mindedness is the opposite of the open heart; the opposite of Christian love. God's love, by contrast, always believes the best of others:

> Love is patient, love is kind, It does not envy, it does not boast, it is not proud. It is not rude, it is not self-seeking, it is not easily angered, it keeps no record of wrongs. Love does not delight in evil but rejoices with the truth. It always protects, always trusts, always hopes, always perseveres. Love never fails. (1 Corinthians 13:4-8a)

If we really believed these verses, it would be a joy to work together with Christians from other denominations and different backgrounds; to learn from individuals and groups who may have different emphases and experiences of the Holy Spirit, of sanctification, of mission and evangelism. Instead, we bicker and fight over these and every conceivable minor issue. I believe strongly that a lack of understanding is a basic cause of this narrow-mindedness, and that it is essential for us to look at these issues that divide Christians with honesty and with love. This is the only way in which we will learn to have a wide open heart.

Labels

Our fondness for putting labels on people, for assuming that people will live up (or down) to our stereotyped image of their spiritual background or denomination, has probably caused more damage than any other issue in the church. For a start, it is harder to generalize now than at any other time in history. There are evangelical people and Bible-believing people and charismatic people in almost every denomination you can find.

Often we criticize; but in fact we are very ignorant of what other people believe. For instance, I know a lot of people who are very negative about the charismatic movement, but, in fact, are very ignorant of what that movement actually means and what it includes.

And what happens to the people who are criticized in a situation like this? Often they in turn become more narrow-minded. Especially if they feel they're under attack, especially if they feel threatened. They react defensively, either by the spoken or written word, in a way that may not help the situation. This is the way divisions and prejudices start. I've made some mistakes in this area myself. I've said some things about people and groups that were perhaps less than best, and sometimes those things have been remembered ever since.

The Word of God teaches that love covers over all wrongs. I strongly recommend that you read *Love Covers* by Billheimer (see page 98). The Word of God also teaches that different Christians can and should have fellowship together. This means that we should know how to compassionately disagree.

Someone asked me recently, "How exactly do you compassionately disagree?" Let me give you an example. Maybe I have a strong conviction that I should wear red socks. Then one day a Christian friend comes to me and says, "Brother, I don't believe you should be wearing those red socks. I believe you should be wearing yellow socks." What do you think I should do in that situation? Do I immediately say, "Yes, my friend, you are right. I see it all now. All these years I have been disobeying God by wearing red socks." Not at all! There is no reason why I should not follow my own convictions in relatively minor matters. Or do I say to my friend, "If that is the way you feel, we can no longer have fellowship together. Until you repent of your yellow socks, I will not work with you." No! He also has the right to his own opinion. Neither do we spend weeks and months ignoring the needs for evangelism,

service and prayer while we argue out the matter of socks. No, we agree to disagree. I still love my friend, I still fellowship with him, and I still work with him, however much we compassionately disagree.

Now I know that this is a very trivial illustration. But I believe that the same principle can apply to many other things that Christians may feel are much more important, although not as important as the basic doctrines such as the divinity of Christ, the inspiration of the Scriptures, and the need for all people to repent and believe. These things, the things that you will find in the doctrinal statement of most evangelical churches or organizations, are basic. But there are many other things that are not basic. And if you are to have anything to do with Operation Mobilization or any other Christian organization, sooner or later you will see things that you don't like. Don't let that hinder you! I see a lot of things in OM that I don't like, and I'm still working with them. My wife sees a lot of things in me that she doesn't like, but she hasn't abandoned me!

Doctrine

Now, says someone, it is all very well learning to compassionately disagree over socks, or hymn books, or orders of service. But what about much more important matters? What about people who deny the lordship of Christ, or the full inspiration of the whole Bible, or the need for mission and evangelism. Surely our attitude to them must be one of absolute rejection!

We are on a narrow road as Bible believing Christians when it comes to these basic beliefs. And it is right that we should have clear in our minds what is a minor, negotiable matter and what is beyond negotiation and debate — the basic beliefs of our faith. It is normal to have struggles with people over these basic teachings; the church in New Testament times was constantly struggling in this area. In some cases we may have to separate from someone, in terms of

working together. I'm not saying that we can always work with everyone. We need to have our principles. We need to have our standards. But when we decide that we can't work with a particular Christian, it doesn't mean that we get arrogant with him; that we become unloving. It means that we compassionately disagree.

We had a big meeting once with a particular group, and we had to make the decision that we would not work together unless they changed their position on a number of areas. The biggest one was that at that time they taught that to be a disciple you had to leave secular work. Nobody was a true disciple unless they left secular work. Now although that is not as fundamental as the divinity of Christ, it was still a basic divergence, because one of the strongest messages in OM is that you can be a disciple back in your home town, working in an office, a factory or a school; wherever God puts you. But we came out of that very difficult meeting with love for one another. And in fact I have continued my friendship with the leader of that group and we've corresponded ever since. Sometimes we need to just let these things go and be past history. Not to hold anything against anybody, just continue to pray and press on with the work.

Most evangelical Christians believe that the Bible, as originally written down, is without error and fully inspired by God's Holy Spirit. Not surprisingly, this is the area where we have the most disagreements with other groups and individuals. But sometimes we need to understand where the problem lies. Some people seem to find it easy to believe every word in the Bible. Personally, I'm always a bit skeptical about how genuine this is. "Oh, God's Word, it's so wonderful; it ministers to me every day;" Christians are always so positive about the Bible.

Nobody ever wants to admit that they have any problems with the Bible; maybe because they don't want to be thought heretics. But I want to tell you that

I have had a lifetime's struggle with it, especially with many passages in the Old Testament. It would be so much easier not to believe that it was inspired by God. Now in fact I do believe that the Bible is God's inerrant word, but I can't say that I've arrived at that belief without a struggle, or without many, many questions and doubts over passages in both the Old and New Testaments.

I have tried to run back to agnosticism. I'm not a natural Christian; I'm a natural backslider. I don't believe things easily. I've wrestled with the doctrine of hell every year since my conversion, trying to reject it, so that I wouldn't have to believe that all these non-believers were lost. It would relieve a lot of spiritual pain, a lot of pressure, to believe that somehow all these good people will make it to God some other way than by hearing and responding to the gospel of Christ.

I have been very greatly helped in this whole area by Dr. Francis Schaeffer. Years ago I listened to a series of tapes by Dr. Schaeffer on this and similar subjects (see page 98), which I found incredibly helpful. There *are* problems for those of us who believe the Bible is God's Word. But I believe the problems are much greater for the man who does not believe the Bible is God's Word.

And once you accept that the whole of the Bible is God's Word, then you need to look at every passage on a particular subject, in context, before you can see what God is saying to us on that subject. You cannot simply base your life on one or two verses on any one subject, taken out of context. And if you take the whole of the Word of God, and let one verse balance out another verse, as we discussed in the last chapter, then I believe you will end up in the land of the open hearted. You will see that God works in different people in different ways, and in different situations in different ways. I am aware, of course, that you can also take certain passages and promote a narrow-minded

viewpoint. But to do that you have to take some verses and leave out other verses. Let's take the whole of the word of God and enlarge our vision of what God is doing today.

The Holy Spirit

The second large area of disagreement and narrow-mindedness among Christians is over the work of the Holy Spirit in our lives. This is particularly ironical since the Holy Spirit was given to the church so that we could be united and so that we could love one another; so that we might have power to witness; so that we might have a Teacher and a Guide. Perhaps when you look at things from the devil's point of view it is not surprising that he has used this issue to divide and confuse Christian people.

It is essential to understand that many of our present divisions over the work of the Holy Spirit have arisen from deep, historical differences in the theology between the different branches of the Protestant church. Now this is not the time or the place to go into these different theologies, although if this is troubling you, you could write to me in care of the publishers and I will send you a book list. All that you need to understand here is that some churches emphasize very strongly the sovereignty of God and therefore that when people become Christians, they are baptized with the Holy Spirit at that point, and are then saved for eternity. They are filled with the Holy Spirit day by day if they are walking with God and learning to do his will. The churches that emphasize this point of view tend to be those known as 'reformed' and include many Presbyterian, Baptist and Free Evangelical churches.

Other churches (including the Methodist and Holiness churches) emphasize much more man's free will, and believe that once a person becomes a Christian, it is then necessary to seek the 'second blessing' or filling or baptism of the Holy Spirit (here these terms are taken to mean the same thing) as a separate experience. They

believe that Christians have the Holy Spirit at conversion, but that they must be filled with the Spirit to receive power to work for God, and that if they turn away from God their salvation may even be lost. Historically Pentecostal and charismatic Christians have followed on from this line of theology, but they emphasize the 'baptism of the Spirit' as a much more dramatic experience usually involving speaking in tongues. They also tend to emphasize the other supernatural gifts of the Spirit, such as healing, more than other churches.

Where it gets complicated is that in these days charismatic churches have arisen from all sorts of denominations, so that you may get charismatic Methodists, charismatic Baptists, or charismatic Anglicans, as well as the 'house churches' and 'community churches'. Most of these groups are very strongly evangelical, and are similar to the Pentecostal churches on their views of the Holy Spirit, although their teaching on other issues, such as church government, is usually quite different. Of course there are many, many variations between all the different groups and between different individual churches, so we must be careful not to generalize about any individual's beliefs.

All evangelical believers agree that the essential thing is that we must be born again. Now some people have tremendously emotional conversions, others have quiet conversion experiences; others are not even sure when they were born again. Are people from the first group going to say that the others have never been born again? Of course not! We can see clearly that God sometimes works like a mighty rushing wind, and sometimes like a still, small voice. But in both cases, the important thing is to remember that God is working in different ways in different people.

I believe that the same is true of the rest of the Christian life. God works in different people in different ways. God can fill you with His Spirit, if you are from the reformed tradition, like me, day by day as you

walk with Him. Or He can fill you dramatically in what some would call a 'crisis experience'. Billy Graham says of the filling of the Holy Spirit, "I don't care how you get it: just get it!" Today we are spending a lot of time arguing about words, about the language we use to describe how the Holy Spirit works in other people's lives, instead of getting on and letting Him work in *our* lives.

Does God only use people from one stream of theology? No, of course not. You only have to read any history of missions to see that some of the greatest men and women of God have come out of one or the other of these schools of thought. And they all lived lives in the power of the Spirit.

In fact if you read some of the biographies of these great men of God you will soon see that the lives of the one group were as powerful as that of the other group. Wesley, the founder of Methodism, was completely opposite in his theology of the Holy Spirit to Whitefield, the great preacher, and yet God used them both in the great Evangelical Revival in Britain. I wish we had a few men like this now, whatever they believed about sanctification. I wouldn't bother asking Wesley or Whitefield what he believed about the work of the Holy Spirit, before I decided whether I could work with him. I can work with anyone who has such spiritual reality in his life.

Fruit and Gifts

I believe we need to make an important distinction between the fruit of the Spirit and the gifts of the Spirit. The fruit of the Spirit is produced in all Christians as they yield to the Holy Spirit, as we saw in the first chapter. I believe that once a Christian has been truly filled with the Holy Spirit, however that filling has come about, the fruit of the Spirit will be seen in his or her life.

> The fruit of the Spirit is love, joy, peace, patience, kindness, goodness, faithfulness, gentleness and self-control. (Galatians 5 :22-23a)

This is why I am not that concerned whether you have had a thunderbolt experience of the Holy Spirit or a 'still, small voice' experience. I am convinced that the important thing is what you are *today* in terms of holiness. Is the fruit of the Spirit present in your life each day, and in increasing power?

The fruit of the Spirit should be produced in every Christian as he or she yields to the Holy Spirit. But the gifts are given according to the will of God. He may give one to one person and half a dozen to another! He may even give different gifts to different people at different times in their lives!

I do not believe that we should try to tie God down, and insist that unless Christians have the gift of tongues or prophecy or healing or whatever, that they are not filled with the Holy Spirit. It seems to me that to be so dogmatic about what gifts individual Christians should have, and to try to impose those ideas on others from different backgrounds and different traditions, is not biblical and, indeed, undermines the sovereignty of God in our lives.

> Are all apostles? Are all prophets? Are all teachers? Do all work miracles? Do all have gifts of healing? Do all speak in tongues? Do all interpret? But eagerly desire the greater gifts.
> (1 Corinthians 12:29-31)

What are these greater gifts? Love is the greatest gift of the Holy Spirit, as Paul goes on to show us in 1 Corinthians 13.

Extremism

Going on from divisions among Christians over the work of the Holy Spirit leads us on to look at the position of extremists in the church. Among extremists I include those from all streams of theology, whose

beliefs, if carried to extremes, may become dangerous heresies.

For example, Christians may believe in the sovereignty of God. But if they start to take that belief to the extreme, and to believe in the sovereignty of God to such an extent that they take away completely the free will of man, they will deny any need to tell people about the good news of Jesus Christ! "If God wants to save the heathen," they will say, "He will save them. Don't get excited about it. The whole world is in His hands!"

Other Christians may believe strongly in the need to be 'baptized in the Spirit' to give power to witness. But if they are not careful, they may become extreme about the need for 'spiritual experience' or 'revival' and spend all their time in emotionally-charged meetings rather than getting on with the work for which the Spirit was sent.

I have met some Christians who seem to see demons everywhere, and may end up getting themselves into situations they are unable to handle. Every time they see a sick person they think, 'Demons!' Now if you see someone who is truly demon-possessed, the thing to do is to fast and pray and to ask the advice of a more mature Christian or Christian leader. Please do not think that you personally must rescue every person with deep problems.

Some Christians become extreme over the question of healing. Now I know that God can heal the sick. I know that He can raise the dead! I believe God can do anything! I personally have seen sick people raised back to health after praying for them. But that does not mean that we should be so taken up with prayer that we forget to call in a properly qualified medical person, whose gifts of healing also come from God.

Sometimes I meet people who get 'guidance' from God through visions and dreams. Now, God's method of guidance is His Word, the Bible. I don't doubt that

in some cases He may give a vision to someone... but that vision *must* be in accordance with the Word of God. I am also very hesitant about putting a lot of emphasis on God speaking to us through dreams — although I know that in the Middle East we have seen God use dreams very powerfully to turn Muslims to Christ.

How important it is to realize that when we start taking verses out of context we can defend almost anything! No matter what you are doing, you are in trouble when you begin to trust only in your feelings, and then try to justify those feelings from the Scriptures. God says that we are to love Him with all our heart, soul, mind and strength. This includes the emotions, of course, but it also includes our reason and our common sense.

I believe that it is nothing less than a miracle, the way young people in OM from many, many churches and backgrounds have worked together in unity for all these years, with almost no serious division. Truly, only the Holy Spirit of God working in people's hearts could have done the impossible!

But Satan will try to take any Christian organization, even OM, and make it extreme on some point or other. I tell you, *anything,* no matter how good, taken to an extreme, becomes a snare. And if we become unloving, and narrow-minded, and start to judge and condemn each other, then we are going to grieve the Spirit of God.

But when we learn to open our hearts to God to be filled with His Spirit — *then* the world is going to shake! It is this that will bring people into a realistic experience of Jesus Christ.

Dogmatism

It is truly amazing what Christian people can find to disagree on. I have been to public seminars where you sit and listen to two Christian speakers arguing with each other quite strongly; sometimes on an

important issue, but other times on completely trivial matters.

One Christian leader in America has decided that all televisions are idols, just as there were idols in the Old Testament. And this group of Christians took their 'idols' into the back yard and they took out their guns (I don't know what they were doing as Christians carrying guns, that seems to be quite acceptable in America) and they blew up their televisions. Militant Christianity! Yet another leader has declared that all contemporary Christian music, particularly if it has a beat (I don't know how you decide whether or not it has a beat), comes from the pit of Satan.

In his book *Love Covers,* (see page 98) Billheimer talks about the tremendous divisions that arose between the old Holiness Christians and the new charismatic Christians. He found it very difficult, as an old Holiness man, to accept these American charismatics as Christians, when he saw the way they dressed and the way the women used make-up. The old Holiness Christians believed make-up was from Satan! These issues divided families and split churches down the middle. And to this day, churches are splitting over things like this, and best friends are turning on each other.

I have run into storms in this area myself. Once, when I was very young and very ignorant, I showed a set of slides about our evangelistic campaigns in Mexico in a very strong Holiness church, and one of them was a slide of my aunt's house, and she had a pair of shorts on. So I said, "Oh, on the way to Mexico for our campaign, we stayed with these Christian people;" (I didn't want to say my aunt) "and we had fellowship with them." That was the end of my fellowship with that church! The pastor took me into a corner afterwards and he said, "I have been fighting shorts for over five years and you have come in here and in twenty minutes undone what I have tried to do for five years."

I was just a young Christian: I didn't know shorts were of the devil!

When I was younger, one of my areas of very great dogmatism concerned drinking, as a believer, any form of alcoholic beverage. I had a message against alcohol when I was only seventeen that was considered right out of the prohibition era. People compared me with Billy Sunday, who used to smash bottles of whiskey in the pulpit during his sermons. And I was convinced that a dedicated believer and a teetotaller were the same.

Then I came to Europe; to Spain. I was longing to see some of the Spanish Christians moving into full time Christian work, because there was so much for them to do. I was very excited when God answered our prayers, and delighted when one of these Spanish disciples came to me and invited me over to his house for lunch. And there they were, pouring out into glasses...WINE!

Of course, I soon discovered that even the most committed Spanish believers have wine at their tables, and they regard it as a really minor issue. But to me it was not minor! I wrestled with this issue to the point of torture! But in the end I had to accept that people from different backgrounds could have different beliefs, and still work together in love.

Separation

One of the biggest issues at present in the American fundamentalist church is that of separation. Many of the American separatist Christians have turned against Billy Graham, and they have also turned against us in OM, because they regard us as being part of the ecumenical movement, which is part of the movement of Antichrist.

Now I believe in separation; from apostasy, from heresy, from sin! But what we're talking about here are double-separated Christians; that is, people who believe in secondary separation. This means that if I

were to have lunch with a Christian friend (even though I may not agree fully with all his views), and he in turn has shaken hands with a theologian who once denied the Virgin Birth, then I would also be tarnished by that theologian's views, so if you were a true double-separated believer you would not be able to have fellowship with me.

Now you may not have heard of this issue before; you may think this is something quite small and unimportant. But this is one of the biggest issues in the American church, without any question. There was one Christian who was one of the most outspoken voices of this particular brand of Christianity, who conducted city wide evangelistic campaigns with only double-separated Christians. But after many years of conducting these campaigns, God showed him how unloving, how narrow-minded and rigid he had been, and he decided that he had to leave.

He then wrote an article explaining why he was leaving, which hit the fundamentalist world in America like an atomic bomb. Because he had been so involved he was able to expose all the bickering and the negative criticism that took place in these supposedly super-separated Christians. Indeed, he compared it to a KGB operation in which people and organizations are listed and black listed, according to whether they can be considered truly separated or not.

This issue has caused a lot of hurt and a lot of pain. And that has been felt even out on the mission field. I thank God that the heart of that Christian leader was opened, and that he has written letters of apology to many of the people that he had previously spoken against. I believe that God was able to bring him out of that cul-de-sac of rigidity because of his great love of the Word of God. He had memorized so much of the Bible that the Holy Spirit did indeed lead him back to the truth and to a more open heart.

Organizations

Yet another area that divides Christians is the tension between the local church and other Christian organizations, often described as 'para-church'. This affects us in OM, because some people who would benefit both themselves and others by working with us for a time do not come, because they or their churches 'don't believe in para-church organizations'. They believe that all mission should be carried out by the local church. When it comes to sending people overseas, of course, the local churches generally do not have the experience or structures necessary to do this —and so often very little results.

The work of God is bigger than any fellowship or organization. Often, to get a particular job done, God has raised up organizations or mission societies. They have been brought into being to meet a specific need. We don't worship the organization, we don't get up-tight because we don't agree with every single thing in that organization. We need to think about the picture of the Body in 1 Corinthians 12:

> The eye cannot say to the hand, "I don't need you!" And the head cannot say to the feet, "I don't need you!" (verse 21)

God has brought into being movements like OM as a response to a specific need. We have a planet of five billion people, with huge churches around America and Europe, and many young people in these churches, at least when we began our work, were sitting around doing nothing. So God said, "These people need to move!" And by His mercy He raised up a movement that has expertise and gifts in mobilizing and training and recruiting people, and now those people (over forty thousand young people have now had training in OM) are working with almost every mission society in the world today.

But still some churches and groups believe that all para-church organizations (such as SERVE, or OM, or

YWAM, or TEAR Fund) are not really of God, or are somehow God's second best. They believe (as we do) that God works through the local church. But they seem to see para-church agencies as somehow in opposition or competition to the local church, whereas we believe that they should be subject to the local church. Recently we have seen signs that this attitude is changing, and we look forward to the time when we will be able to work with all these churches, as an overseas agency to carry out the work of evangelism for and with the local church. We believe that one of the greatest keys to the evangelism of the world is partnership, and we long for that to increase.

Let's stop bickering and judging and criticizing the way things are done in this movement or that organization. Let's praise God for the work that all these different agencies are doing; those that specialize in relief work, those that specialize in outreach, those that specialize in long term mission and those that specialize in short term training. As we thrust ourselves into reaching many, many people around the world who have never yet responded to the gospel, I believe we're going to need one another; we're going to need unity. And I believe that as we become more united, we'll be able to pray together in spiritual power; and as we pray together in spiritual power, then we'll be able to tear down the strongholds of the enemy.

An Open Heart

So I want to plead with you, on the basis of these passages we have considered, and on the basis of many, many other passages throughout the Bible, to have a wide open heart. Work with all of God's people. Learn to love them. And when someone initially turns you off, go back to your room and say, "Jesus, I believe you're going to do a work in my heart towards that person." And sometimes the greatest fellowship you have will be with people who are very, very different from you.

You may even be surprised and end up marrying someone who's very different from you! I can tell you, there's nothing like discovering, as a hard-line fundamentalist from a good reformed background, several years after your marriage, that your wife is praying privately in tongues in another room! And I am convinced that through unity and through love we don't have to sacrifice basic truth; we don't have to compromise our deep personal convictions. But through love we can operate and live and function in a way that will provide less scandal for the outside community and bring more glory to God.

Lord, we pray that unity may increase in Your Body, and that we would have enlarged vision, more open hearts, more open minds; not to bring in error, but to keep things in their right perspective by the power of your Holy Spirit. Grant us this as we go forward together, often struggling with very many basic issues in life, but students of Your Word and committed to world evangelism.

Amen.

4

Real People, Real Power

HOW REAL IS YOUR CHRISTIANITY? Is it the sort of discipleship that Jesus talked about when He said,

> "If anyone would come after me, he must deny himself and take up his cross daily, and follow me. For whoever wants to save his life will lose it, but whoever loses his life for me will save it."
> (Luke 9:23)

Or are we, in the words of A.W. Tozer, that great man of God who many called a twentieth century prophet, simply "serving our own interests under a disguise of godliness" (see page 98)? Instead of belonging to the local sports club, or social club, we belong to the church. There we find meetings with like-minded people at regular times (but not too often or there will be complaints), pleasant and uplifting music and even rewarding times of helping others.

But the Christian life is not firstly about more meetings, or more songs. The Christian life is about justice and peace and righteousness and godliness and purity. It's reaching out to your neighbor, at convenient times and inconvenient times. It's helping him when he has a flat tire. It's helping him when he needs

to get to the hospital. It's not firstly about giving money, it's about giving chunks of your life. And until we start practicing that, we know very little of what Jesus meant when He talked about being a disciple.

Being a Disciple

What does Jesus mean in these verses by denying ourselves and taking up a cross? It is clear that He is not talking simply about giving up chocolate for Lent, or even a 'hunger lunch' where money saved on food goes to the starving. He is talking about a continual, daily process.

When Jesus died on the cross for us, He paid the price for the sin of our own hearts. It was that sin which had enslaved and corrupted us. And so, to follow Him into deliverance, we need to be saved from ourselves, from our sinful nature and self-centeredness. Only as we deny self daily are we freed from its domination.

So it is our own selves, our own nature, that we are to deny and put to death. For the cross Jesus is talking about here is not some golden ornament to decorate our churches, but an instrument of death. Only as we take up that cross daily, identifying ourselves with Jesus' death to all that is opposed to the will of God, will we be delivered from ourselves.

Now you may say that all this talk of denial and death is old fashioned and negative. But it is only through that denial and daily death that true life begins. True, the cross is the end of a life of sin and slavery; but it is also the beginning of a life of holiness and spiritual revolution. When Jesus says 'follow me' He is not calling us to a narrow, negative existence, but to the most exciting and beautiful fellowship you could ever dream of.

The Crucified Life

I believe that God is calling every Christian to this life of self-denial and commitment. Jesus said,

> "Anyone who does not carry his cross and follow me cannot be my disciple." Luke 14:27)

To carry a cross and follow your Lord does not make you into some kind of religious freak. I believe that we can all have a deeper commitment, that we can be filled with the Holy Spirit, and that Christ can be Lord of every area of our lives, and yet that this can happen in a very sane, down-to-earth, balanced and God-glorifying way. I believe that it is possible for us to be genuine and sincere in our Christian lives without becoming overly emotional or introspective.

Why is it that so often, when Christians talk about the need for repentance and the good news of Jesus Christ, they are ignored by the world around? There are many reasons, but I am sorry to say that one of the most common reasons is that we do not live what we preach. We preach a gospel of love, and yet we do not love each other. We preach a gospel of commitment, and yet we ourselves are not committed. And the man or woman in the street is not deceived by our fine words and religious phrases. It is only when the people around us see the evidence of a changed life that they will begin to take what we say seriously.

The key to reaching people with the gospel is not evangelism at home or abroad, not serving others in the church or in the community (although all these things are part of the gospel), but it is the changed hearts of Christians. The key is for Christians to allow God to take over their lives; putting self to death and letting Jesus rule instead. We may spend all the hours we like in evangelism and service, but unless our hearts have changed we will be doing it for ourselves, and not truly serving God.

To change the whole direction of our lives in this way may hurt at the time. A man of God once said, "In the Christian life there'll be no gain without pain." No wonder so few are really going on for God today! We are the generation that has run away from pain more than any other generation; we've got every medicine

in the world, every kind of painkiller you can imagine. But there's no painkiller you can take that's going to take away the pain of spiritual growth.

Roy Hession in his book *Calvary Road* (see page 98) talks about the need for brokenness before God, the need for coming to a place where we realize that our lives without Him are totally worthless, and that we are dependent on Him for everything. These ideas are not very popular today. But when God begins to break down the hard core of pride, selfishness and arrogance in your heart, it's going to hurt. Are you prepared for that? Can you really sing, "Break me, melt me, mold me, fill me" and mean it? Because God will answer your prayer, if you mean it from the heart.

Let's look now at four very practical ways in which we can make sure that Jesus is really Lord of our lives.

1. Letting Jesus be Lord of our relationships. Have you had any really good messages in your church lately on sex? There are over five or six hundred verses in the Bible on the subject of sex that we almost never preach on, but you can be sure that if anyone gets into sexual sin, they will be gossiped about and they will be looked down upon, and they will have a rough time among all the nice respectable Christians.

When we see people fall into sin who are part of the church, we should realize that part of the responsibility is ours. Because we have not taught on this subject, we have not taught our young people how to have healthy relationships with the opposite sex, we have not taught them how to withstand temptation and have a realistic view of sex and marriage. Instead we watch more romantic films and we read more romance books than any other generation in history, and we're paying an awesome price for it in broken marriages and broken families, as people find that their expectations of married life do not add up to the reality. I'm not saying there's no place for romance, but I'm saying that the whole thing has gotten out of control.

Billly Graham said that if you don't win this battle against impurity, you lose the biggest battle in the Christian life. And I know there are people all over the world, though they may be leaders, though they may love Jesus, who are walking in sin in the area of impurity. Every time I've ever spoken in a conference people have come up to me for prayer or they have written to me and they've confessed sex before marriage or other kinds of immorality or pornography that's been tearing them apart and turning them into a spiritual split personality.

Paul, two thousand years ago, wrote to Timothy, and he said, "Flee the evil desires of youth"(2 Timothy 2:22). In other words, if you are young and you have a girlfriend or a boyfriend, you don't drive off in your parent's car to watch the sunset alone together on a hot summer evening, and then pray that God will make your thoughts pure. If you take your girlfriend or your boyfriend, however many years they have been Christians, and you go alone into the dark corners, the college bedrooms or the back of a car, you are asking for trouble. No — instead you "flee the evil desires of youth". You keep in the company of others, you take advantage of social events and sporting events, and you build up a friendship and a spiritual relationship that will keep you following God together in the years to come.

In the middle of all the news recently about the immorality going on among Christian leaders, my daughter came to me one day and said, "Dad, I want to know whether you have been faithful to Mother for all the time you have been married." Now I have battled with lust all my life; even before my conversion at the age of sixteen I was addicted to pornography, and had already had over a dozen girlfriends (fortunately that was in the age of romance, rather than permissive sex). So it was one of the greatest joys in my life to be able to tell my daughter that by God's grace and by denying self and taking up my cross daily to follow Jesus, I had indeed been faithful to my wife for all of these twenty-eight years.

I am hesitant to tell that story, but I think that it's important to realize that the media generally likes to report only the negative things. And for every Christian leader who falls, there are dozens and dozens who learn the basic principles of discipleship; who learn the disciplined life, the crucified life, who know how to stand against temptation, and who are therefore running the race with Jesus day by day.

2. Letting Jesus be Lord of our words. Is your tongue controlled by the Spirit of God? The Psalmist was so conscious of his need for control that he said,

> "Set a guard over my mouth, O Lord;
> keep watch over the door of my lips."
> (Psalm 141:3)

Uncontrolled words have destroyed more churches and more families, I believe, than immorality, crime or lying. Destructive gossip is one of the most potent forces for evil in the Christian world today. Because every time you repeat a rumor, every time you spread a little tidbit of negative comment about a fellow Christian or Christian group, you are dividing and hurting the Body of Christ. And this has been one of Satan's most effective strategies in recent years.

There is a place for talking on a trivial level, particularly with neighbors and non-Christian friends. Let us beware of becoming so superspiritual that we can only reply with a Bible verse when a neighbor makes some comment on the weather. Our neighbors need to know that we are real, sane people, and that we too are concerned with what concerns them.

And there is a place for constructive criticism, preferably made to the person concerned, face to face. But so often what most of us do is to gossip. We are afraid to confront people who have irritated us, people who have hurt us, people whom we believe are behaving wrongly. So instead of going to them and, in love, telling them how we feel, we let all our bitterness and anger out to our friends. And they pass it on to their friends, who pass it on to their

friends. Eventually, of course, it gets back to the original people concerned, but by then it is so exaggerated and negative that they find it very, very difficult to forgive. And so you get division and bitterness arising in the church.

Now unless you have learned, as a spiritually mature person, to have some control in this area, then you are not ready to use your tongue to tell people even in your own culture about the gospel, let alone launch out into cross-cultural evangelism. Because the potential for misunderstandings in other languages and cultures is very, very great. The work of God can be put back for years or even decades in a sensitive situation by someone with an uncontrolled and undisciplined tongue.

Learn to think before you speak. Learn to know what Jesus would have said to that person, in that situation. Whatever the temptation to seem right, or clever, or simply to have the last word, it is our determination to deny self and follow the Lord in this area that will make the difference.

3. Letting Jesus be Lord of our time. Time, it is often said, is our most precious asset. Not one of us knows how much of it we have left, or what will be God's plan for the rest of our lives. Yet when we let Jesus have true control of our lives, we will not necessarily end up doing more. Many of us spend far too much time already in religious activity. We seem to be convinced that the more time we spend, the better our service for the Lord must be. So we rush around like whirlwinds, blissfully unaware that we are victims of our own undisciplined and disorganized lives. We are always 'too busy', and yet actually we accomplish very little.

Many years ago, I was in danger of becoming a little extreme on this particular issue. I felt I should always get up in the morning by 6:30 a.m., and if I slept later than this, even if I had been late to bed the night before, I felt that I should somehow work harder to make up for the lost time. Also, I personally did not

feel that I had the time to relax or play sport, because the demands were so overwhelming. And God had to show me that He was in control, and that occasionally a little extra time sleeping, or a couple of hours playing golf, or even an evening to take my wife to a movie, could all be included in His plan.

Tozer says, "Working for Christ has today been accepted as the ultimate test of godliness among all but a few evangelical Christians. Christ has become a project to be promoted instead of a Lord to be obeyed... The result is an army of men who will run without being sent and speak without being commanded" (see page 98).

Let us make Jesus truly Lord of our time, thinking about the priorities of what we have to do from His perspective, not ours (and that may bring about some changes that will surprise us) and organizing our time for maximum efficiency and speed. Let us keep calm and relaxed, knowing that He is always in control and that no so-called 'last minute crisis' is beyond His power and grace.

4. Letting Jesus be Lord of our finances. "Any of you who does not give up everything he has," said Jesus, "cannot be my disciple" (Luke 14:33). This is not a popular verse today. For many people, financial security is an important and overriding ambition. We have already seen the absolute importance of surrendering everything we possess to God. Now let us think about letting Him be Lord of every aspect of our finances.

For instance, should your choice of career be motivated by the financial security it will bring? Or is your security in the Lord of heaven and earth? This is not to say that He may not guide you into a well-paid career. The rich have greater responsibilities in the kingdom of God. We will see in the last chapter how great is the need for more senders, more supporters, in world missions today. A lack of finance is limiting the work of God today in every place I have ever visited.

Is Jesus Lord of all your possessions? Have you laid them at His feet, asking Him which you truly need and which you should sell or give away? Many Christians today seem to follow unquestioningly the materialist idea that every year they should own more and more. But this is not God's way. God supplies according to our needs, and if you no longer need what God once gave you, I believe you should think seriously about whether you should still keep it. Equally, we must learn not to hanker after things simply because our neighbors have them. Our priority should be to glorify God, not to keep up with those next door.

Most Christians today know very little about trusting God for their everyday needs. In the nineteenth century George Müller supported not only himself and his family but hundreds of orphans on the answers to prayer alone (see page 98). He said that if we want great faith we must begin to use the little faith we already have. Dare today to trust God for something small and ordinary, and next week or next year you may be able to trust Him for answers bordering on the miraculous. Many people who have come on Operation Mobilization campaigns over the years have found that having to trust God for day-to-day finances has transformed their attitude to money and possessions. If He is really Lord of all we have, we need not feel guilty about what He has given us, but can use it wisely and sacrificially in His work.

A Deeper Commitment

"If any man would come after me," said Jesus; and in this one phrase He put before us the choice that has divided the world ever since. Do we really want to follow Him or is the cost too great? If we really want to become followers of Christ we must become personally involved in His death and resurrection; through repentance, prayer, self-denial, humility, obedience and sacrificial love. That is why it is easier to talk about commitment than to experience it.

The cost of true commitment is indeed great. But the rewards are even greater. It is only when we take Jesus' words seriously, and act upon them, that His power breaks through into our lives.

Let's realize that the crucified life is for everyone. We are all called to purity, to reality. We are all to be keen to spread God's word. Is it wrong for me to think that every Christian should be excited about Jesus, the Son of the living God? He is living in our hearts, making us kings and priests and heirs of His kingdom.

It's because I believe that God has called every Christian to a life of deeper commitment and true discipleship that I am involved in a training program like OM. If you come with OM you won't study for a degree or spend all your time in books or essays or debates, although there will be opportunity for all those things. Instead our programs have been patterned on the methods that Jesus Christ used. Jesus' training was on the job. His disciples were doers, not just hearers. And they learned as much by their mistakes as by their successes.

In OM we expect young people to move out in evangelism, in prayer and in team living. And quite soon they start to find out what the crucified life is all about. Because there's nothing like a few real problems of insufficient finance or food you don't like or simply a team member you can't get on with to bring out the areas in your life which are not yet controlled by the Holy Spirit.

Now I'm not saying that spiritual growth is going to happen overnight. And I want to make it clear that we are learners, and we are strugglers. We are like the learner drivers in Britain with their 'L' plates displayed for everyone to see. And yet it's as we are willing to learn that God leads us on to a deeper commitment and a Spirit-filled life.

Pray your own prayer of surrender. Pray a prayer of repentance, come to Jesus in faith, and breathe in

that forgiveness and that grace and renewal that the Holy Spirit can give. And determine to be a spiritual fighter, a spiritual runner, a disciple of Jesus Christ.

Let the Holy Spirit fill you. Trust God's word; God has not given us a spirit of fear but of love and power and a calm mind. Some of us need to understand more of what it is to take a deep drink of the grace of God. I need the grace of God, the forgiveness, and the mercy of God every day. And I have found that often God meets us in the moment of weakness, rather than strength. He doesn't always wait until we feel spiritual, He doesn't always wrap life up in a nice little present with a bow on the top. The life of discipleship, the life of deeper commitment includes ongoing battles and ongoing struggles. It will include fear and worry and anxiety at times. But Jesus is always there.

I believe God is waiting for you to make the greatest, deepest commitment and surrender of your life to Christ, and His Word, and His cause, that you have ever made. I believe He's waiting for you to put your hands on the plow and determine you're not going back. Whether He leads you to Hong Kong, Pakistan or New York City; whether He leads you into 'full-time' ministry or whether He leads you to be a hard working sender supplying the desperately needed finance.

Do you love Jesus? Do you love Jesus with all your heart, soul, mind and strength? Have you put your life on the altar as we're told to do in Romans 12:1-2, "I urge you, brothers, in view of God's mercy, to offer your bodies as living sacrifices"?

Yes, this is a lifetime challenge. You may say it is too much. But I want to say on the authority of God's Word that it's not too much. Because God gives grace. He forgives when you fall down. He lifts you up. He cleanses, He renews, He forgives. He knows all about you, and He loves you still. It's that love that should motivate us to give our lives more fully to Him in total commitment and surrender, and be the real people that God would have us to be.

Commitment is part of a process; if you're not willing to deny self daily, take up the cross and follow Jesus; if you're not willing to put into practice the principles of the crucified life, then the initial commitment, even if made for a second or third time in your life, will be of little value. Praise God for the experience that you may have as the Holy Spirit works in your life and blesses you and fills you, but if that crisis is not followed by a process it will become an abscess.

I believe many people are ready for God's process. I believe the Holy Spirit is preparing many people for steps forward in their Christian lives. He may even have prepared you, if you want to say with all your heart, "I am crucified with Christ, I will surrender everything to Him, I'll go where He wants me to go and do what He wants me to do."

Living God, byYour Spirit, convict us of areas where we're fooling around. Convict us of areas of laziness. Convict us of the barriers we've built up around ourselves. May self be crucified; may You be magnified, as we consider the challenge before us, as we consider the spiritual harvest field. We, O Lord, want to be real people. We thank You for real power, the power of Your Holy Spirit, who lives and remains in us. We thank You for the power of the gospel, which is Your power, O God, for salvation. We thank you, Lord, for the dayYou saved us and set us free. We thank You for this great gift of salvation.

Lord, we hunger and thirst for reality, that what we say we believe will be a burning fire in our hearts and in our lives. May we take steps of faith to be Your men, to be Your women, to go where You want us to go and to do what You want us to do. We thank You, Lord, for Your forgiveness and Your grace that can make all of this possible.

In Jesus' name,

Amen.

5

Accepting Yourself and Others

JESUS SAID, "Love your neighbor as yourself." If you have never learned to love yourself you will find it very difficult to love others as Jesus commanded. Accepting yourself is not a once-for-all experience, but something you will learn gradually, often through struggles and failures.

You were created in God's image. And part of His creation was your particular personality, your appearance and even your background; all those things that you cannot change and that make you into the individual you are. God does not make mistakes. He knew you even before you were born;

> My frame was not hidden from you
> when I was made in the secret place.
> When I was woven together in the depths of
> the earth,
> Your eyes saw my unformed body.
> All the days ordained for me were written in
> your book
> Before one of them came to be.
>
> (Psalm 139:15-16)

So God knows how He can work in you and through you and with you. To doubt that God can use you is to doubt His power. Believing that God made you as you are is the first step to self-acceptance.

God's purpose for your life is not to destroy your personality; instead, He wants to enrich it. Being filled with God's Spirit doesn't mean you can't enjoy a sunset any more; it doesn't mean you won't get excited about music or pizza; it doesn't mean that you won't fall in love, that your heart won't pound or your eyes pop when that someone special comes into view. But it does mean that a very powerful degree of self-control will come into your life, so that you will be able to sort out the priorities, the difference between your God-given personality and your selfish nature, so that you will be able to say 'no' to self and 'yes' to Jesus.

It took me a long time before I slowly, gradually, began to accept myself as God had made me. I had this image of what a really spiritual person should be like —very quiet and yet powerful— and I just did not fit that image at all. I even went as far as trying to dress in a way that I felt people expected, in a dark suit and tie. But gradually I realized that God could use me as I am.

You may find that your particular personality means that you don't feel comfortable with certain churches or groups or organizations. You may appreciate them, you may agree fully with what they are doing, but you feel you will never fit in with them. This is not a matter of spirituality but of personality. Sometimes God may ask you to work with them despite that, and sometimes it will be agreed by everyone that it would be better if you worked with another group.

I am very aware that Operation Mobilization is not everybody's cup of tea. God has raised us up as a unique fellowship, to carry on a unique task. We have to train people in a specific way. When I was in Pakistan, I met some of our men and women in OM Pakistan who are learning Urdu. That takes extra

discipline. That takes perhaps a degree of soldiering and perseverance that working in America may not necessarily demand; here you probably have other problems, for which we need other qualities. We're all different. We all have different amounts of energy, we all have different gifts. Be yourself; don't try to be somebody else.

God's Purpose

It is important to understand why God has created us as we are; with our own particular personality, appearance and background. He has something planned for our lives which can only be done by someone with that particular combination of characteristics. His plan for your life cannot be fulfilled by any other individual on this earth.

Many of us may feel that we are too weak for God to use us. But it is through these weaknesses that God's power is revealed in our lives. The apostle Paul was told clearly by God,

> "My grace is sufficient for you, for my power is made perfect in weakness." (2 Corinthians 12:9)

We all need to learn this principle. Often in Christian work we look for the attractive person, or the clever person, to be in our group. We need to learn to work with the weak, the unattractive, the slow, for this is how God works.

Remember also that God has not yet finished His work in you. However long you have been a Christian, whatever sort of training you have been through, God has only just started in His lifetime process of making you more like Jesus Christ. Let us learn to look forward to what God is going to do in our lives, rather than always looking back.

Think of your outward appearance as a picture frame that shows off the inner qualities and Christlikeness that God is developing in your life. Your inner self, the picture of your personality developed

in fellowship with God, is the greatest advertisement possible for the gospel of Jesus Christ. Jesus said,

> "Let your light shine before men, that they may see your good deeds and praise your Father in heaven." (Matthew 5:16).

If you are allowing God to develop genuine qualities of love and humility in your life, even though you may not feel He has got very far yet, these will be recognized by unbelievers.

If you find it difficult to accept yourself as you are, or if you find in your heart bitterness or resentment against God for your background or the way you are, ask God to forgive you and help you. Some people have more problems in this area than others. Those who have come from difficult or unloving homes can have real problems relating to God as a loving heavenly Father.

The Human Factor

If we believe that God has made our personality, then we need to allow room for the development of that personality in our lives. This is something that is often overlooked in Christian circles. We must allow for the human factor or, no matter how 'spiritual' we become, we will not survive the tests and challenges ahead of us.

Some of the greatest men and women of God in history have had problems in just this area. One of my favorites is Elijah. In 1 Kings, chapter 18, we read that the people of Israel had been turning away from the Lord to follow the false god Baal. So Elijah summoned the prophets of Baal and all the people and the king to Mount Carmel, and challenged them to a contest. Two bulls were placed on wood ready to be sacrificed. Then Elijah told the prophets of Baal to pray:

> "You call on the name of your god, and I will call on the name of the Lord. The god who answers by fire — he is God." (verse 24)

Elijah asked God for a miracle, and God answered him. He prayed and the fire fell, and the people were awestruck. He triumphed over the false prophets, made absolute fools of them, and he became the great hero of Israel. But what did he do next?

Elijah was afraid and ran for his life. When he came to Beersheba in Judah, he left his servant there, while he himself went a day's journey into the desert. He came to a broom tree, sat down under it and prayed that he might die. "I have had enough, Lord," he said. "Take my life; I am no better than my ancestors." Then he lay down under the tree and fell asleep. (1 Kings 19:3-5)

So here is the great prophet, under a tree, thoroughly depressed. I find this story very moving because I see many Christians suffering from depression and sometimes they don't seem to have heard about the examples that we see in the Bible, in these stories of the great men and women of God. Sometimes we think that these things can be answered by the right Bible verse or someone coming up with the right spiritual prescription, and our pride keeps us from actually seeking the help we need.

I praise God that I have seen people effectively treated, medically treated, for some forms of depression. And so I believe that we need to discern when the problem is emotional, or spiritual, or when it may be something physical that will need medical help.

Discouragement is a normal part of the Christian life. It is part of our human nature. Some people get discouraged more easily than others, and some get depressed more seriously than others. But if you are active for God and you're allowing God's word to challenge you, and you're being used even a little by God, then sooner or later you will go through times of discouragement. And it seems that if discouragement is a normal part of human experience, then as Christians the important thing is to know how to handle it.

I believe that discouragement is the most common strategy that Satan uses to reduce the effectiveness of Christians today. And part of the battle against discouragement is won when we realize that this is something that many, many Christians and Christian leaders have been through before us.

I have treated the subject of discouragement more thoroughly in my book *No Turning Back* (see page 98). Basically, I believe that learning to handle discouragement is part of normal spiritual growth. We should not expect some sort of supernatural deliverance or emotional experience to wipe out all our negative feelings. God has given us His Word, the Bible; we should be feeding on it, and learning the promises of God. He has given us His Son, the Lord Jesus, and put within us the Holy Spirit. It's as we learn to draw upon what we already have in Christ by His Holy Spirit that we will be able to come through discouragement.

Look at God's strategy for discouragement in the story of Elijah. First of all he makes sure that Elijah has had a good sleep. Much discouragement can be put down to sheer physical tiredness. Then an angel brings him food, not once but twice, so that he is fully refreshed and strengthened for what is to come. After all this Elijah is ready to go on in the work of God.

I have found this story tremendously helpful. I have always had the potential to become extreme on a number of issues, and some years ago I began to think that it was wrong for me to spend any time just relaxing and being myself. I looked at the number of people in the world who didn't know Christ, and I looked at the need for prayer and the need for evangelism and I thought that anything else was a waste of time. I was trying to deny the human factor. And God took this verse and showed me that I had to allow time for my own personality if He was going to go on to use me.

I believe that as we learn to trust God more and give ourselves time to relax, we will be able to go on in the

Christian life far more effectively. Let us think of God's race as a marathon rather than a sprint; maybe even an 'ultra' marathon where people run for as many as a thousand miles at a time. If you started a race like that as a sprint you would not get very far. It is the ones who have trained hard and rested well, and who allow enough time to stop to sleep and to eat who can survive that sort of race.

Forgiving Ourselves

Just as we cannot love others if we do not love ourselves, we will find it difficult to forgive others if there is something in our lives for which we have never forgiven ourselves. We may have confessed it to God, and been forgiven. But instead of then forgiving ourselves we feel we must suffer for the sin, whatever it is, and try to work it out in a sort of self-imposed purgatory.

If you know there is something in your life that you have never forgiven yourself for, first make sure that you have asked for God's forgiveness. Then make sure that you have made things right with the other people involved. For instance, if you have stolen money, even if it is a very small amount, it is not enough to ask God's forgiveness. You must also return the money.

Many of us will go to almost any lengths to avoid going to someone and asking forgiveness. It is amazing what excuses our pride can find for just this simple step. Probably the best thing is to go immediately, as soon as we realize that it is necessary, without thinking too much about it. However, do take care to be sensitive and not to make things worse by speaking in the wrong way.

Sometimes Christians seem to feel that they should not apologize or admit past sins to non-Christians. In fact this is one of the most powerful messages a Christian can bring. Non-Christian people do not like apologizing either, and they will realize that your faith

must mean a lot to you if you are prepared to bury your pride and admit you have been wrong.

Accepting Others

The very process of learning to accept ourselves will take us some way towards accepting others, as we recognize some of the struggles they may be going through. However, there are bound to be some times of conflict when we feel another Christian has hurt us, and this can lead to deep-seated resentment and bitterness if we do not react in a Christ-like way.

If you feel that someone has hurt you, keep calm and rational. Try to understand the situation and what caused it. Could you have prevented it? How do the other people involved feel? Try to concentrate on kindness and love for them, rather than your own hurt.

Make sure that you have forgiven anyone who has hurt you. Then leave the hurt alone for it to heal. Do not dwell on it and the way you have been wronged, or bitterness and self-pity will fill you. Do not withdraw from other Christians, even the one who has hurt you, and accept apologies if they are offered.

Forgiving Others

We should forgive others as we have been forgiven by God:

> Peter came to Jesus and asked, "Lord, how many times shall I forgive my brother when he sins against me? Up to seven times?
>
> Jesus answered, "I tell you, not seven times, but seventy seven times." (Matthew 18:21-22)

Forgiveness is as basic to our Christian living as the cross of Jesus Christ is to the plan of salvation. Forgiving others means that we believe that God is in control. He is the one who should judge and punish, if necessary, not us.

A lack of forgiveness can lead to many problems in our lives. Bitterness may result in tension, inability to sleep and even psychosomatic illness. It will stop our spiritual growth, causing an inability to love God, doubts about our own salvation, and a bad witness to others. It is not surprising that depression may be the end result.

> If anyone says, "I love God," yet hates his brother, he is a liar. For anyone who does not love his brother, whom he has seen, cannot love God, whom he has not seen. (1 John 4:20)

If you find it difficult to forgive some people, realize that all the hurt you have experienced may be God's way of pointing out their need. They may have deep-seated problems that they are unable to deal with, and that have caused them to hurt others. God may now be leading you to do what you can to help. Pray for them, help them, be friendly, and if you have hurt them ask their forgiveness. This may help them to realize that they also need to ask your forgiveness. Paul wrote to the Christians in Rome:

> Do not repay anyone evil for evil.... If it is possible, as far as it depends on you, live at peace with everyone. Do not take revenge, my friends, but leave room for God's wrath, for it is written: "It is mine to avenge; I will repay," says the Lord. On the contrary:
>
> "If your enemy is hungry, feed him; if he is thirsty, give him something to drink.
>
> In doing this, you will heap burning coals on his head."
>
> Do not be overcome by evil, but overcome evil with good. (Romans 12:17-21)

So let us make these principles a reality in our hearts. Let us learn to accept ourselves and others in all the complexity that God has created, listening to God and waiting for His voice. Let us learn to thank God for what He has already done in our lives and for what He is going to do, allowing Him to fill us afresh

each day with His Holy Spirit, so that we can go where He wants us to go and do what He wants us to do.

Lord, You know all about us and You love us still. We thank You that we have been accepted by You and that is the basis of our acceptance of ourselves. You love us with an everlasting love; if we were the only one on the planet You would still have sent Your Son to die on the cross for us. We thank you that Your arms reach out to embrace us. Draw us in. Deliver us, Lord, from lack of self-acceptance. Deliver us from living in unbelief. We yield ourselves to You and we believe that You can and will do a new thing in our hearts, in our lives, in our churches, as we move forward by faith, learning to love ourselves and others as You love us, that in the years to come we may still be running, still be praying, still be praising, still be learning.

In Jesus' name,

Amen

6

New Generation — Unfinished Task

WHAT PART ARE YOU PLAYING in God's plan for the world?

God's plan for the world did not finish with the crucifixion and the resurrection. It is now carried on through His Church, as we are indwelt with the Holy Spirit on a day by day basis. It will lead to nothing less than the birth of the living Church in every nation and people group. It will also lead to healing and God-centered change on every level of society.

This task of world evangelism and spiritual revolution has been committed to all of us who know Him and are His disciples. There are no spectators. We are all to be in the battlefield and a part of the action.

Jesus, before He left this earth, told us of the task we are to complete and gave us a promise to take with us:

> "All authority in heaven and on earth has been given to me. Therefore go and make disciples of all nations, baptizing them in the name of the Father and of the Son and of the Holy Spirit, and

> teaching them to obey everything I have commanded you. And surely I will be with you always, to the very end of the age."
>
> (Matthew 28:18-20)

This task that Jesus gave us is not some afterthought of His ministry, but is the logical outcome and culmination of the whole of His life and work. Its emphasis is not just on preaching but on making disciples, and on teaching obedience. And His command to make disciples of all nations is to all of us. It is not just to a few who feel 'called', or to Christian leaders or Bible college graduates. We all have a part to play in God's plan of reconciliation. And His promise to be with us always is to be claimed as we go forward in faith to obey His commands.

The Task

Patrick Johnstone, in his prayer handbook *Operation World* (see page 98), estimates the size of the task that lies before us. First of all we have to think of those who have never even heard the gospel. Out of the approximately five billion people who made up the world's population in 1986, there were between one and two billion who had never heard about the need for repentance and the good news of Jesus Christ. There were also between three and four thousand people groups who had no church or Christian fellowship of their own, and these groups range from small minorities to quite large nations.

You may have heard in the news recently about the Kurds; one of the largest unreached people groups in the world. There are approximately twenty million Kurds who no longer have their own political nation; instead they are split up mostly between the nations of Iran, Iraq and Turkey. They were very badly affected by the chemical warfare in the Iran/Iraq war. They are just one of dozens of other unreached people groups I could tell you about; all of these are covered in the prayer requests in *Operation World*.

Patrick Johnstone also reminds us that each new generation must be evangelized afresh: God has no grandchildren. Each person, whether they come from a Christian family or not, must respond to the message of Christ. This means that the whole task facing us is enormous. So how can anyone say that the day of world missions is past?

To get the job done, if we are serious about following the commands of Christ, there must be an increase in the Church's witness worldwide that is at least in line with the increase in world population. This is the task we are facing. Jesus' words have never been more revelant, "The harvest is plentiful but the workers are few" (Matthew 9:37). In many, many areas of the world people are crying out for a Christian witness, and we must ask ourselves why they have none.

Now I am not convinced that it is the will of God for so many people groups to have no witness. It follows, therefore, that some or many of us are not playing our part in God's plan; we are not carrying out God's complete will, whether it be to pray or to send or to go. We cannot blame it all on God any more than William Carey, the first Baptist missionary to India, could when people told him so many years ago, "If God wants the heathen to be saved, then He will take care of it without the likes of you." It is God's plan as revealed in His Word that these people hear the gospel; that they receive a witness.

The challenge of world evangelism is as great today as it ever was. We can use any number of missionaries, if they are Spirit-controlled, and Spirit-guided, committed men and women. As we see the opportunities that are before us, I believe that there are unlimited possibilities for long term and short term service.

The methods: Long Term

Our objective is to witness to the whole world, whether people respond to the message or not. Obviously we must constantly re-evaluate what we are doing and

always try to improve the way we communicate to people, and also pray strongly that they will respond. But we must not give up and go home just because people in some areas are slow to understand the message and follow Christ.

We must understand that there may be many reasons why people do not respond. This is why Operation Mobilization has been able to tackle the evangelism of Muslims, where there has been very little response, because we have men and women who stick to the task. In some cases our missionaries have been working in Turkey, which is a mainly Muslim country, for almost twenty-five years. And still, after years of patient and sensitive evangelism, there are less than a thousand indigenous believers in Turkey (and most of these are from minority ethnic groups).

Jesus said; "My food is to do the will of Him who sent me and to finish His work" (John 4:34). Our first objective must be not to see how many we can convert, but to obey God. I believe we need to learn about stickability. Paul says in the letter to the Corinthians, "Stand firm. Let nothing move you. Always give yourselves fully to the work of the Lord, because you know that your labor in the Lord is not in vain" (1 Corinthians 15:58). And in the letter to the Galatians he backs that up; "Let us not become weary in doing good, for at the proper time we will reap a harvest if we do not give up" (Galatians 6:9).

Now in that sort of situation, where it's not possible to turn the leadership of the mission over to the national church, because there is no national church, and it may take several years to learn the language and the culture, we need long term missionaries. We need people who are prepared to make cross-cultural communication their career, to study it and work at it for many years. We need people who can remember that they are servants and that their objective is not ultimately to lead the nationals but to make it possible for the nationals to lead themselves.

Such people are rare, and we treasure every one of them. In many specialized missions, such as hospitals, schools and those which concentrate on pastoral training and teaching, long term missionaries are also needed. They provide continuity, language and communication skills, and much needed experience and spiritual maturity.

The Methods: Short Term

However, many Christians seem to have got the idea that these long term missionaries, with their high levels of gift and grace and training, are the only sort of missionaries that are needed. I read a book recently saying that if we had more short term missionaries they would only get in the way of the career missionaries and the national church. Some Christian leaders have written off all short term missionary work as 'superficial'.

Now this seems to me to be limiting God. Many people who may not have the grace and the gift to be a long term career missionary learning Urdu or Arabic could probably still make a major contribution by giving two years of their lives to being God's soldiers in the overseas spiritual war zone, particularly in areas where there is no other mission and there is no other church.

Young short term workers (and those whose families have grown up) are a practical answer to many of the problems of world missions today. They are able to go out to needy countries at a time of life when they may not have received much training, but neither are they tied down by the family responsibilities of young children or elderly parents. They are also much cheaper to support. These days, the support of a missionary family is beyond the resources of many average-sized churches. So it makes sense to send out young people to gain experience or test a missionary call before they commit themselves to a lifetime overseas.

And the short term worker, whatever his training or lack of it, can play a vital role working under the leadership of the longer-term missionaries and local church. Literature is still a vital way to get the gospel out; you don't need a PhD or a theological education to distribute powerful gospel literature written for the mind and the mentality of the target audience. We can now use films and videos and audio-cassettes, but you need people to drive the vehicle, to run the projector, to cook the food.

We live in a highly technical world. It's not any longer a matter of just getting Bible teachers and theological graduates; they are also needed, but they may be limited in their work without mechanics and engineers and maintenance experts. We need dedicated arms and dedicated eyes.

The big teaching in Britain, the U.S.A. and some other countries now seems to be; go through university, get as many qualifications as you can, get a good job, make money, and then, when you are all settled down, if the Lord leads, you can go to the mission field. Now this sounds fine, but in fact it does not work. Some people do manage it; but most of us, once we are married and settled down with our children, are stuck for life.

It is understandable that with all the changes and pressures that a growing family brings, we are unwilling to take on yet more change and yet more unknowns. And those that do go overseas at this phase of life are usually the ones who have already gotten involved as short term missionaries when they were younger. We should be encouraging our young people to make the most of their flexibility when they have it, so that they can then make informed decisions about where the Lord is leading them and their families later on.

It's about time that we understood the difference between reality and geography. Of course we call people to lifetime commitment. But to give the idea that

people who serve for two years and then return haven't made a lifetime commitment to Jesus Christ is false. Their commitment to Christ is not affected by the country in which they are living.

Of course we need people with a lifetime commitment to serve the Lord overseas. But we shouldn't force people into such a commitment if they're not ready for it, or if their health won't stand it, or those 'lifetime' missionaries will be back home in a year or so anyway. Many of the pioneer missionaries of the last century died within the first few years of their overseas work, but we would hardly write their work off as superficial.

I would like every young (and not-so-young) Christian to consider the possibility, both for their own spiritual growth and in obedience to Scripture, of two years of cross-cultural communication on the spiritual battlefronts around the world today. And let us not be afraid that we're going where we are not wanted. Church leaders are coming to me almost daily, from every area of the world where we are working, and asking, pleading for more workers.

We should take note of the fact that the Mormons have twenty or thirty thousand men on their short term overseas mission program. They have made over a hundred thousand converts in Britain alone. Is that superficial? They let nationals take over the leadership of their groups and continue the teaching they have started, and when the short term missionaries return to America they send another thirty thousand to take their place.

I believe the Church of Jesus Christ should have at least, at any one time (as well as the long term missionary force), a hundred thousand men and women on a one year or two year program. They would not get in the way of each other, or of the national church, if they were trained in a few basic rules of the game; like submitting to the national church leadership, working alongside people, not lording it over them but learning

from them, and making sure that the leadership of any mission or missionary project was transferred to the leadership of the national church as quickly as possible.

The People

What is a missionary? Some people have a vision of a tall white colonial figure in a pith helmet carrying a big black Bible, marching through the jungle, attacking venomous snakes with one blow of his machete and catching hordes of cockroaches with his bare hands and dashing them to the ground. Others imagine an elderly, humorless spinster with a piano accordion teaching little black children to sing "Jesus loves me".

If this picture of a missionary was ever true (which I doubt), it certainly isn't true today. Modern missionaries may be Bible teachers or evangelists or translators, or they may be doctors or nurses or agriculturists or accountants or craft workers. Or they may be mechanics, cooks, secretaries, bookkeepers, electronic engineers, or people who are willing to go anywhere and do anything. They must be prepared to go as learners and servants of Jesus Christ and the national church, being what Patrick Johnstone calls "self-effacing spiritual giants" (see page 98).

If you don't feel you're a missionary type, take heart. I don't feel I'm one either. I sometimes think that I must have been the most reluctant missionary in the whole world. But the lady who prayed for me for three years prayed that I would not only become a Christian but also a missionary, so I didn't really stand a chance. And, in fact, there is room for every type of personality in mission work.

Many people are frightened by the idea that God might want them to serve overseas, even for a year. Their ideas of missionary work seem to be full of horrible insects and eating all kinds of strange food and suffering in extreme climates. But when they

begin to understand the depth of God's love for them and move by faith, many of them discover that they actually enjoy it when they get to these countries.

The true missionary is not some kind of ascetic, who is perpetually pining for his home comforts and his McDonalds hamburgers. In any case, McDonalds are now getting there faster than we are! I have proved myself that on the mission field, in Spain, Belgium, Holland, and then India, in the midst of the battle there are many wonderful and enjoyable aspects of missionary life. It is one of the fullest, most challenging occupations anyone could ever get into.

But don't missionaries have to have a *special* call from God? I don't believe so. I think we're far too inclined to live by feelings rather than faith. A lot of 'missionary calls' are just that: feelings. Now God may at some point give you an experience which may be a turning point in your life. God is working in different people in different ways. Some people have very emotional missionary calls. They can tell you the moment and the hour they were called.

But many of you are never going to get that kind of emotional call, so you might as well stop looking for it. If you still feel you must have it, just write to me. I will send one of my colleagues around to your house and we will show you some slides and play you some inspiring music all evening, and the next morning you will be ready to go. I can assure you that you will probably not get very far! Because those feelings are not going to last. Come the first set of discouragements or the first two years with no apparent results, that great emotional experience is going to wear a bit thin, or maybe be replaced by an equally strong feeling that you ought to drop the whole idea!

It is my experience that many of the people who are doing the greatest work in missions around the world have never had a *special* call. Instead, they have realized that Jesus' command to witness to every nation applies to all of us. They knew that they had some part

to play in God's plan for the world, and they began to ask themselves what it could be. And gradually, through reading the Bible, listening to the advice of mature Christian friends and talking to mission organizations, they discovered that they themselves were needed overseas — maybe for a year, two years, or even a lifetime.

The trouble with expecting a special 'missionary call' from God is that those who do not experience it tend to assume that God does not want them to be involved with missions. And those who do experience it sometimes tend to see themselves as God's gift to that country, rather than as learners and strugglers, until they learn better. Maybe when we all realize that we have our part to play, and that those who send are at least as important as those who go, we will be able to work together in partnership with each other and with the national church.

God Can Use You

Now if you're willing to play a part in God's great plan for this world, you must be ready to count the cost. Because before God can use you to your full potential, you need to learn the basics of discipleship and commitment and the revolution of love and all the other things we have talked about in this book. That involves discipline; it involves having your daily 'quiet time', and memorizing Scripture, and reading good Christian books and listening to good Christian tapes. It involves being committed to your local church. But it also involves leaving room for your own personality to develop, as we discussed in the last chapter. Super-spiritual people do not survive under pressure.

If you spend two years overseas there's a high chance you're never going to be the same once you come back. You'll have seen how God answers prayer, and how the Holy Spirit changes lives, and you'll have caught a glimpse of what God is doing around the world. When people in the church mention mission programs and different countries for prayer, they'll be

talking about real people and friends that you have all over the world. You'll have seen the value of Bible study and memorization, and praying for the world, and surrendering everything to God and depending on him for your everyday needs.

Of course living for God is a day by day walk, and going on OM or any other program doesn't guarantee that you're going to walk with God all your life, in fact it may mean that you become a greater target of Satan's strategies. So you must know how to withstand his temptations.

Making your life available to God to use for His purposes does not end with reading one book or going to one conference or going on a training program for one year. When Jesus spoke about counting the cost of discipleship, He emphasized the need for stickability, telling the story of a man who began to build a tower and did not have the money to finish it.

> Everyone who sees it will ridicule him, saying, "This fellow began to build and was not able to finish." (Luke 14:29-30)

Now if you are going to be able to finish God's marathon race, you will have to learn God's pace for your life. God does not want sprinters, who go incredibly fast but are exhausted after a hundred meters, but marathon runners who can go on and on. Many young people are impatient to know God's will for their life, when it may well be that it is not God's time for them to find out. There may be things you have to learn and experiences you have to go through before you are ready to hear God's call.

The important thing is to go forward in obedience and faith and not feel you have to force the pace, or you will burn out before you have developed your full potential. It's not what you do in the next ten minutes that counts: that's important, but it's what you do tomorrow and next week and next year that really counts. Learn God's pace for your own life. Don't try to run it at someone else's pace.

The Call: to Pray

If we really believe that God answers prayer, if we really believe that God wants us to be involved in reconciling the nations to Himself, then praying for different countries and the work of missions around the world will become a natural part of our lives. Patrick Johnstone says, "without prayer God's plan for the world cannot be achieved" (see page 98).

I find it astonishing that whole churches do not seem to have heard of the idea of interceding for the different countries of the world. How can we gather Sunday after Sunday in our churches, with some of the liveliest, largest church movements in the world, and yet not pray for those nations, those people groups, where the church doesn't exist at all?

I heard about a prayer meeting in an English city recently where 15,000 people came. And yet we are crying out for more workers to go and work with needy churches overseas. Now if you can have a prayer meeting with 15,000 people you should be able to send out 1,500 overseas workers within the next year or two or something is wrong with the praying.

It is completely unscriptural to pray only for ourselves and for our own country. We need the whole word of God. We've got churches that can praise the Lord, and sing choruses, they can have all kinds of wonderful fellowship times, but if you call for an hour of intercession they look at you as if you were some kind of dinosaur.

Often we simply do not have the time in our church meetings for intercession. The space allotted to prayer is so short; even in a prayer meeting we have so much singing and 'sharing' that by the time we get ready to pray it is almost time to go home.

How many churches devote a whole day or a whole evening just to pray? Do we really believe God is listening? Or is it simply that we have never learned how to pray? As a teenager I started the habit of

having half days with God, then days with God; I often went into the hills or the mountains just to pray. Now we need to be careful, of course, that we're not trying to clock up the hours or the number of countries prayed for so that we can feel 'spiritual'; that would be the height of hypocrisy.

My early attempts at getting alone with God weren't all success. I remember once going for a time of prayer in Spain. I had decided that if the Lord Jesus could pray through the night alone, I was going to pray through the night alone. I'd been in nights of prayer with other people, but there you get somebody else praying and it helps keep you awake. So in great boldness I went outside the city of Madrid for this night of prayer, and I'd also decided to fast, so I brought a piece of bread with me that I thought I would eat in the morning when I'd finished breaking through Satan's strongholds and claiming Spain for Christ (this was under Franco and we needed a lot of prayer, I can tell you).

But it didn't work. About two o'clock in the morning I fell asleep out there by the river. Of course it's very hot in the day in Spain, but it got very cold at night and I wasn't dressed for it, having not really understood this. So eventually I woke up, freezing cold, and decided I was going to eat. I looked round for my bread, but it was gone. To this day I don't know what happened. I think perhaps a wild animal came along, looked at me, didn't see much meat, and took the bread instead!

Don't be discouraged because you fail in your prayer life. Don't be discouraged because your mind wanders. Beware of becoming impatient with your spiritual growth rate. Don't feel you're an extra evil person because in a prayer meeting some amazing young woman or man walks in and blows all your circuits.

Some people think that that kind of experience just happens to the young carnal Christian, but I can tell you from personal experience that it can happen to

anybody. A beautiful girl walked into a prayer meeting in Switzerland a few years ago, and I could not think straight, let alone pray. Eventually, though, the Lord helped me to bring my mind under control in that prayer meeting and now I can't even remember what she looked like.

The Call: to Send

When God called the leaders of the church in Antioch of Syria to send out the apostle Paul and Barnabas as missionaries overseas (Acts 13:2-3), He gave them an important task. They laid their hands on Barnabas and Paul and sent them off, but they were not forgotten. They prayed for their missionaries, sent them all the financial support they could spare, and, most importantly, they continued to support Paul and Barnabas as part of their church family. When the two missionaries returned after several years, their eager reception shown by the Christians in Antioch vividly demonstrated their love for each other (Acts 14:26-28).

Was the role of the Christians who stayed in Antioch less important, in spiritual terms, than that of their two missionaries overseas? It may have been less dramatic, less in the public eye. But their role was no less vital to the work of the mission, because without their support it is doubtful if it would have succeeded. If they had not recognized their responsibilities, the whole of history might have been different. Christians, even the apostle Paul, are not meant to work in isolation, but as part of the Body of Christ.

Our aim as senders is simple; to accept responsibility for those we send out and to love and support them as members of our own spiritual family. That means loving them as we love ourselves; thinking when they need a letter, when they need prayer, when they need warm clothes or new shoes for their children; when they need a birthday card or a little extra money for a special treat. When we send missionaries out, whether or not we knew them personally before they went out, we take on

a partnership with them in the work of God. It is up to us to keep our side of the bargain.

Financial support is, of course, essential. Put simply, if ten Christians give one-tenth of their income to missionary work, they will probably be able to support one missionary. But many church members simply cannot afford to give one-tenth; others do not see the need. And missionaries have families, and the work itself is expensive. So less and less workers can be sent out.

It is not easy to be a dedicated sender in today's affluent society. When all around us are living only for pleasure, it takes courage to be different and to persevere in playing our part in God's plan. And yet that part has never been more essential.

In a world where millions are starving, where tens of millions have no homes, where evangelists in India are praying that they might have a bicycle (and some have been praying for years), we Christians in the affluent society have, I believe, failed to understand Christ's demands upon our lives. Luke 14:33 is very clear: "In the same way, any of you who does not give up everything he has cannot be my disciple."

Those who support and love and pray are not 'second-class missionaries'; indeed, if there is going to be a powerful missionary outflow, there must be a return to the revolutionary standards of Jesus Christ and of the New Testament church.

Maybe you feel that God wants you to be a sender but you don't know anyone who wants to be sent. Don't worry. Write to any mission society, particularly short term organizations like OM or the less 'glamorous' areas like the home bases, and I guarantee you will find people who are trying to obey God's call to go out but are being hindered by lack of support.

I believe that if you let God have his way in your life, if you follow the Spirit of God day by day through difficulty, through trials, and through discouragement,

then you will be part of God's great plan to build His kingdom around the world.

The Call: to Go

Are you willing to respond to God's call to go? If God began to show you that your part in His plan was to leave your comfortable home and church and career for the unknown, even if just for a few weeks or a year, would you be willing to go?

Why are we afraid of God's direction for our lives? When the government called for men to go into the army for the Second World War and the Vietnam war, there were plenty of volunteers and people counted it a privilege to be in the army.

People were not afraid in Iran in the recent Iran/Iraq war, when hundreds and thousands of men and women volunteered to be martyrs, and eleven-year-olds were sent across the minefields to personally blow up the mines with their feet. Their mothers danced at their funerals because they had given another son to Allah, so great is the fanaticism of modern-day Islam.

I wonder if there are some today who would be willing to go out across the devil's minefields, spiritually speaking; maybe risk your future, or that lovely retirement program you've already been thinking about; maybe risk even your life or your health, that one more nation might hear the gospel, that one more unreached people group might have a Christian witness, that one more soul might be with God in eternity.

If we believe in the word of God, the ministry of the Lord Jesus and the power of the Holy Spirit, let us commit ourselves to reach the unreached, to take the gospel to every nation and every people group and to every individual. Let us commit ourselves to be His witness in these places, and also through prayer and faith to see living churches born in each one of these people groups that can multiply and reach the rest of that people group with the Word of God.

If you go out even for only two years and disciple a few nationals who know the language already and carry on in that country for twenty or thirty years planting churches, then you will know the joy of working together with God.

Will anybody remember your name in some far-off land twenty years from now? Will there be one Christian, one church, that's following Jesus because you obeyed, because you were willing to make the sacrifice, because you were willing to take God at His Word? Maybe one day, when you reach eternity, you will discover that one of the people you told about the gospel or prayed for became a believer. And he or she in turn obeyed God and told the gospel to another person. And that person also became a Christian and then brought to Jesus someone who became a great evangelist, and brought thousands of people to Jesus.

It's the ricochet effect; the multiplication effect, the teamwork principle, the domino effect with the Holy Spirit pushing the dominoes. It's one of the most exciting principles you can ever get involved in. Will you do that? Will you begin to take some steps of faith? Will you be honest about where you really are spiritually, and learn to repent of those things that are holding you back, so that as you pray with others you may begin to go forward with God?

I challenge you to be a marathon runner for God in this great task of world evangelism. And when you're knocked down, just get up, and get back in the race and start running. When you fail, when you fall, get up! As soon as you feel your hand touch the ground, get up! And you'll discover that some day, twenty or thirty years from now, just like me, you'll be still running the race; weary sometimes, wounded sometimes, but still pressing on for Jesus Christ. Let's press on together for the kingdom of God and world evangelism.

O Lord, as we come to You, we ask You to make this great vision of reaching all people with the gospel real

to us. Lord, we believe by faith that it can come to pass. We realize that we have a part to play in Your great plan for the world. We know that the final decision is ours; that You will take us so far, lovingly pushing and drawing us, but that the ultimate step to be a doer instead of a hearer must always be ours.

Help us to take it.

Amen.

Bibliography

Love Covers by P. Billheimer, Christian Literature Crusade, 1981.

The Calvary Road / Be Filled Now by R. Hession, Christian Literature Crusade, 1988 (new combined edition)

Operation World by P. Johnstone, STL Books / Zondervan, 1993.

Audio-cassettes by Dr. Francis Schaffer available from:
Rosie Laverton
L'Abri Cassettes
Manor House
Greatham
Liss
Hanats
England, GV33 6HF
Tel: 04207-436

A Living Reality by R. Steer, (Life of George Muller) Hodder & Stoughton / STL Books, 1985

The Set of the Sail by A.W. Tozer, STL Books / Christian Publications, 1986

No Turning Back by George Verwer, OM Literature.

Most of the books listed are still in print and can be obtained from your local bookstore, or, in case of difficulty, from O.M. Literature, P.O. Box 1047, Waynesboro, GA 30830-2047. Tel. 1-800-733-5907.